SOCIAL ANARCHISM OR LIFESTYLE ANARCHISM

AN UNBRIDGEABLE CHASM

Murray Bookchin

Library of Congress Cataloging-in-Publication Data

Bookchin, Murray, 1921–
    Social anarchism or lifestyle anarchism : the
unbridgeable chasm / by Murray Bookchin.
        p. cm.
    Includes bibliographical references.
    ISBN 1-873176-83-X (pbk.)
    1. Anarchism. 2. Social problems. 3. Individualism. 4.
Personalism.
    HX833.B635 1995
    320.5'7—dc20   95-41903
                                                        CIP

British Library Cataloguing in Publication Data

A catalogue record for this title is available from the British Library.

First published in 1995 by

AK Press   AK Press
22 Lutton Place   P.O. Box 40682
Edinburgh, Scotland   San Francisco, CA
EH8 9PE   94140-0682

The publication of this volume was in part made possible by
the generosity of Stefan Andreas Store, Chris Atton, Andy
Hibbs, Stephen John Adams, and the Friends of AK Press.

Typeset and design donated by Freddie Baer.

CONTENTS

A NOTE TO THE READER

This short work was written to deal with the fact that anarchism stands at a turning point in its long and turbulent history.

At a time when popular distrust of the state has reached extraordinary proportions in many countries; when the division of society among a handful of opulently wealthy individuals and corporations contrasts sharply with the growing impoverishment of millions of people on a scale unprecedented since the Great Depression decade; when the intensity of exploitation has forced people in growing numbers to accept a work week of a length typical of the last century — anarchists have formed neither a coherent program nor a revolutionary organization to provide a direction for the mass discontent that contemporary society is creating.

Instead, this discontent is being absorbed by political reactionaries and channeled into hostility toward ethnic minorities, immigrants, and the poor and marginal, such as single mothers, the homeless, the elderly, and even environmentalists, who are being depicted as the principal sources of contemporary social problems.

The failure of anarchists — or, at least, of many self-styled anarchists — to reach a potentially huge body of supporters stems not only from the sense of powerlessness that permeates millions of people today. It is due in no small measure to the changes that have occurred among many anarchists over the past two decades. Like it or not, thousands of self-styled anarchists have slowly surrendered the social core of anarchist ideas to the all-pervasive Yuppie and New Age personalism that marks this decadent, bourgeoisified era. In a very real sense, they are no longer socialists — the advocates of a communally oriented libertarian society — and they eschew any serious commitment to an organized, programmatically coherent *social* confrontation with the existing order. In growing numbers, they have followed the largely middle-class trend of the time into a decadent personalism in the name of their sovereign "autonomy," a queasy mysticism in the name of "intuitionism," and a prelapsarian vision of history in the name of "primitivism." Indeed, capitalism itself has been mystified by many self-styled anarchists into an abstractly conceived "industrial society," and the various oppressions that it inflicts upon society have been grossly imputed to the impact of "technology," not the underlying social relationships between capital and labor, structured around an all-pervasive marketplace economy that has penetrated into every sphere of life, from culture to friendships and family. The tendency of many anarchists to root the ills of society in "civilization" rather than in capital and hierarchy, in the "megamachine" rather than in the commodification of life, and in shadowy "simulations" rather than in the very tangible tyranny of material want and exploitation is not unlike bourgeois apologias for "downsizing" in modern corporations today as the product of "technological advances" rather than of the bourgeoisie's insatiable appetite for profit.

My emphasis in the pages that follow concerns the steady withdrawal of self-styled anarchists these days from the social domain that formed the principal arena of earlier anarchists, such as anarchosyndicalists and revolutionary libertarian communists, into episodic adventures that eschew any organizational commitment and intellectual coherence — and, more disturbingly, into a crude egotism that feeds on the larger cultural decadence of present-day bourgeois society.

Anarchists, to be sure, can justly celebrate the fact that they have long sought complete sexual freedom, the aestheticization of everyday life, and the liberation of humanity from the oppressive psychic constraints that have denied humanity its full sensual as well as intellectual freedom. For my own part, as the author of "Desire and Need" some thirty years ago, I can only applaud Emma Goldman's demand that she does not want a revolution unless she can dance to it — and, as my Wobbly parents once added early in this century, one in which they cannot sing.

But at the very least, they demanded a revolution — a *social* revolution — without which these aesthetic and psychological goals could not be achieved for humanity as a whole. And they made *this* basic revolutionary endeavor central to all their hopes and ideals. Regrettably, this revolutionary endeavor, indeed the high-minded idealism and class consciousness on which it rests, is central to fewer and fewer of the self-styled anarchists I encounter today. It is precisely the revolutionary social outlook, so basic to the definition of a *social* anarchism, with all its theoretical and organization underpinnings, that I wish to recover in the critical examination of *life-style* anarchism that occupies the pages that follow. Unless I am gravely mistaken — as I hope I am — -the revolutionary and social goals of anarchism are suffering far-reaching erosion to a point where the word *anarchy* will become part of the chic bourgeois vocabulary of the coming century — naughty, rebellious, insouciant, but deliciously safe.

— July 12, 1995

SOCIAL ANARCHISM OR LIFESTYLE ANARCHISM

FOR SOME TWO CENTURIES, anarchism — a very ecumenical body of anti-authoritarian ideas — developed in the tension between two basically contradictory tendencies: a personalistic commitment to individual *autonomy* and a collectivist commitment to social *freedom*. These tendencies have by no means been reconciled in the history of libertarian thought. Indeed, for much of the last century, they simply coexisted within anarchism as a minimalist credo of opposition to the State rather than as a maximalist credo that articulated the kind of new society that had to be created in its place.

Which is not to say that various schools of anarchism did not advocate very specific forms of social organization, albeit often markedly at variance with one another. Essentially, however, anarchism as a whole advanced what Isaiah Berlin has called "negative freedom," that is to say, a formal "freedom *from*," rather than a substantive "freedom *to*." Indeed, anarchism often celebrated its commitment to negative freedom as evidence of its own pluralism, ideological tolerance, or creativity — or even, as more than one recent postmodernist celebrant has argued, its incoherence.

Anarchism's failure to resolve this tension, to articulate the relationship of the individual to the collective, and to enunciate the historical circumstances that would make possible a stateless anarchic society produced problems in anarchist thought that remain unresolved to this day. Pierre Joseph Proudhon, more than many anarchists of his day, attempted to formulate a fairly concrete image of a libertarian society. Based on contracts, essentially between small producers, cooperatives, and communes, Proudhon's vision was redolent of the provincial craft world into which he was born. But his attempt to meld a *patroniste*, often patriarchal notion of liberty with contractual social arrangements was lacking in depth. The craftsman, cooperative, and commune, relating to one another on bourgeois contractual terms of equity or justice rather than on the communist terms of ability and needs, reflected the artisan's bias for personal autonomy, leaving any moral commitment to a collective undefined beyond the good intentions of its members.

Indeed, Proudhon's famous declaration that "whoever puts his hand on me to govern me is an usurper and a tyrant; I declare him my enemy" strongly tilts toward a personalistic, negative freedom that overshadows his opposition to oppressive social institutions and the vision of an anarchist society that he projected. His statement easily blends into William Godwin's distinctly individualistic declaration: "There is but one power to which I can yield a heartfelt obedience, the decision of my own understanding, the dictates of my own conscience." Godwin's appeal to the "authority" of *his* own understanding and conscience, like Proudhon's condemnation of the "hand" that threatens to restrict *his* liberty, gave anarchism an immensely individualistic thrust.

Compelling as such declarations may be — and in the United States they have won considerable admiration from the so-called libertarian (more accurately, proprietarian) right, with its avowals of "free" enterprise — they reveal an anarchism very much at odds with itself. By contrast, Michael Bakunin and Peter Kropotkin held essentially collectivist views — in Kropotkin's case, explicitly communist ones. Bakunin emphatically prioritized the social over the individual. Society, he writes,

> antedates and at the same time survives every human individual, being in this respect like Nature itself. It is eternal like Nature, or rather, having been born upon our earth, it will last as long as the earth. A radical revolt against society would therefore be just as impossible for man as a revolt against Nature, human society being nothing else but the last great manifestation or creation of Nature upon this earth. And an individual who would want to rebel against society . . . would place himself beyond the pale of real existence.[1]

Bakunin often expressed his opposition to the individualistic trend in liberalism and anarchism with considerable polemical emphasis. Although society is "indebted to individuals," he wrote in a relatively mild statement, the formation of the individual is social:

> even the most wretched individual of our present society could not exist and develop without the cumulative social efforts of countless generations. Thus the individual, his freedom and reason, are the products of society, and not vice versa: society is not the product of individuals comprising it; and the higher, the more fully the individual is developed, the greater his freedom — and the more he is the product of society, the more does he receive from society and the greater his debt to it.[2]

Kropotkin, for his part, retained this collectivistic emphasis with remarkable consistency. In what was probably his most widely read work, his *Encyclopaedia Britannica* essay on "Anarchism," Kropotkin distinctly located the economic conceptions of anarchism on the "left-wing" of "all socialisms," calling for the radical abolition of private property and the State in "the spirit of local and personal initiative, and of free federation from the simple to the compound, *in lieu of* the present hierarchy from the center to the periphery." Kropotkin's works on ethics, in fact, include a sustained critique of liberalistic attempts to counterpose the individual to society, indeed to subordinate society to the individual or ego. He placed himself squarely in the socialist tradition. His anarchocommunism, predicated on advances in technology and increased productivity, became a prevailing libertarian ideology in the 1890s, steadily elbowing out collectivist notions of distribution based on equity. Anarchists, "in common with most socialists," Kropotkin emphasized, recognized the need for "periods of accelerated evolution which are called revolutions," ultimately yielding a society based on federations of "every township or commune of the local groups of producers and consumers."[3]

With the emergence of anarchosyndicalism and anarchocommunism in the late nineteenth and early twentieth century, the need to resolve the tension between the individualist and the collectivist tendencies essentially became moot.* Anarcho-individualism was largely marginalized by mass socialistic workers' movements, of which most anarchists considered themselves the left wing. In an era of stormy social upheaval, marked by the rise of a mass working-class movement that culminated in the 1930s and the Spanish Revolution, anarchosyndicalists and anarchocommunists, no less than Marxists, considered anarcho-individualism to be petty-bourgeois exotica. They often attacked it quite directly as a middle-class indulgence, rooted far more in liberalism than in anarchism.

The period hardly allowed individualists, in the name of their "uniqueness," to ignore the need for energetic revolutionary forms of organization with coherent and compelling programs. Far from indulging in Max Stirner's metaphysics of the ego and its "uniqueness," anarchist activists required a basic theoretical, discursive, and programmatically oriented literature, a need that was filled by, among others, Kropotkin's *The Conquest of Bread* (London, 1913), Diego Abad de Santillán's *El organismo económico de la revolución* (Barcelona, 1936), and G. P. Maximoff's *The Political Philosophy of Bakunin* (English publication in 1953, three years after Maximoff's death; the date of original compilation, not provided in the English translation, may have been years, even decades earlier). No Stirnerite "Union of Egoists," to my knowledge, ever rose to prominence — even assuming such a union could be established and survive the "uniqueness" of its egocentric participants.

INDIVIDUALIST ANARCHISM AND REACTION

To be sure, ideological individualism did not fade away altogether during this period of sweeping social unrest. A sizable reservoir of individualist anarchists, especially in the Anglo-

---

* Anarchosyndicalism can be traced back, in fact, to notions of a "Grand Holiday" or general strike proposed by the English Chartists. Among Spanish anarchists, it already was an accepted practice by the 1880s, a decade or so before it was spelled out as a doctrine in France.

American world, were nourished by the ideas of John Locke and John Stuart Mill, as well as Stirner himself. Home-grown individualists with varying degrees of commitment to libertarian views littered the anarchist horizon. In practice, anarcho-individualism attracted precisely *individuals*, from Benjamin Tucker in the United States, an adherent of a quaint version of free competition, to Federica Montseny in Spain, who often honored her Stirnerite beliefs in the breach. Despite their avowals of an anarchocommunist ideology, Nietzscheans like Emma Goldman remained cheek to jowl in spirit with individualists.

Hardly any anarcho-individualists exercised an influence on the emerging working class. They expressed their opposition in uniquely personal forms, especially in fiery tracts, outrageous behavior, and aberrant lifestyles in the cultural ghettos of fin de siècle New York, Paris, and London. As a credo, individualist anarchism remained largely a bohemian lifestyle, most conspicuous in its demands for sexual freedom ("free love") and enamored of innovations in art, behavior, and clothing.

It was in times of severe social repression and deadening social quiescence that individualist anarchists came to the foreground of libertarian activity — and then primarily as terrorists. In France, Spain, and the United States, individualistic anarchists committed acts of terrorism that gave anarchism its reputation as a violently sinister conspiracy. Those who became terrorists were less often libertarian socialists or communists than desperate men and women who used weapons and explosives to protest the injustices and philistinism of their time, putatively in the name of "propaganda of the deed." Most often, however, individualist anarchism expressed itself in culturally defiant behavior. It came to prominence in anarchism precisely to the degree that anarchists lost their connection with a viable public sphere.

Today's reactionary social context greatly explains the emergence of a phenomenon in Euro-American anarchism that cannot be ignored: the spread of individualist anarchism. In a time when even respectable forms of socialism are in pell-mell retreat from principles that might in any way be construed as radical, issues of lifestyle are once again supplanting social action and revolutionary politics in anarchism. In the traditionally individualist-liberal United States and Britain, the 1990s are awash in self-styled anarchists who — their flamboyant radical rhetoric aside — are cultivating a latter-day anarcho-individualism that I will call *lifestyle anarchism*. Its preoccupations with the ego and its uniqueness and its polymorphous concepts of resistance are steadily eroding the socialistic character of the libertarian tradition. No less than Marxism and other socialisms, anarchism can be profoundly influenced by the bourgeois environment it professes to oppose, with the result that the growing "inwardness" and narcissism of the yuppie generation have left their mark upon many avowed radicals. Ad hoc adventurism, personal bravura, an aversion to theory oddly akin to the antirational biases of postmodernism, celebrations of theoretical incoherence (pluralism), a basically apolitical and anti-organizational commitment to imagination, desire, and ecstasy, and an intensely self-oriented enchantment of everyday life, reflect the toll that social reaction has taken on Euro-American anarchism over the past two decades.*

During the 1970s, writes Katinka Matson, the compiler of a compendium of techniques for personal psychological development, there occurred "a remarkable change in the way we perceive ourselves in the world. The 1960s," she continues, "saw a preoccupation with political activism, Vietnam, ecology, be-ins, communes, drugs, etc. Today we are turning inward: we are looking for personal definition, personal improvement, personal achievement, and personal enlightenment."[4] Matson's noxious little bestiary, compiled for *Psychology Today* magazine, covers every technique from acupuncture to the *I Ching*, from est to zone therapy. In retrospect, she might well have included lifestyle anarchism in her compendium of inward-looking soporifics, most of which foster ideas of individual autonomy rather

---

*For all its shortcomings, the anarchic counterculture during the early part of the hectic 1960s was often intensely political and cast expressions like desire and ecstasy in eminently social terms, often deriding the personalistic tendencies of the later Woodstock generation. The transformation of the "youth culture," as it was originally called, from the birth of the civil rights and peace movements to Woodstock and Altamont, with its emphasis on a purely self-indulgent form of "pleasure," is reflected in Dylan's devolution from "Blowin' in the Wind" to "Sad-Eyed Lady of the Lowlands."

than social freedom. Psychotherapy in all its mutations cultivates an inwardly directed "self" that seeks autonomy in a quiescent psychological condition of emotional self-sufficiency — not the socially involved self denoted by freedom. In lifestyle anarchism as in psychotherapy, the ego is counterposed to the collective; the self, to society; the personal, to the communal.

The ego — more precisely, its incarnation in various lifestyles — has become an *idée fixe* for many post-1960s anarchists, who are losing contact with the need for an organized, collectivistic, programmatic opposition to the existing social order. Invertebrate "protests," directionless escapades, self-assertions, and a very personal "recolonization" of everyday life parallel the psychotherapeutic, New Age, self-oriented lifestyles of bored baby boomers and members of Generation X. Today, what passes for anarchism in America and increasingly in Europe is little more than an introspective personalism that denigrates responsible social commitment; an encounter group variously renamed a "collective" or an "affinity group"; a state of mind that arrogantly derides structure, organization, and public involvement; and a playground for juvenile antics.

Consciously or not, many lifestyle anarchists articulate Michel Foucault's approach of "personal insurrection" rather than social revolution, premised as it is on an ambiguous and cosmic critique of power as such rather than on a demand for the *institutionalized* empowerment of the oppressed in popular assemblies, councils, and/or confederations. To the extent that this trend rules out the real possibility of social revolution — either as an "impossibility" or as an "imaginary" — it vitiates socialistic or communistic anarchism in a fundamental sense. Indeed, Foucault fosters a perspective that "resistance is never in a position of exteriority in relation to power. . . . Hence there is no single [read: universal] locus of great Refusal, no soul of revolt, source of all rebellions, or pure law of the revolutionary." Caught as we all are in the ubiquitous embrace of a power so cosmic that, Foucault's overstatements and equivocations aside, resistance becomes entirely polymorphous, we drift futilely between the "solitary" and the "rampant."[5] His meandering ideas come down to the notion that resistance must necessarily be a guerrilla war that is always present — and that is inevitably defeated.

Lifestyle, like individualist, anarchism bears a disdain for theory, with mystical, and primitivistic filiations that are generally too vague, intuitional, and even antirational to analyze directly. They are more properly symptoms than causes of the general drift toward a sanctification of the self as a refuge from the existing social malaise. Nonetheless, largely personalistic anarchisms still have certain muddy theoretical premises that lend themselves to critical examination.

Their ideological pedigree is basically liberal, grounded in the myth of the fully autonomous individual whose claims to self-sovereignty are validated by axiomatic "natural rights," "intrinsic worth," or, on a more sophisticated level, an intuited Kantian transcendental ego that is generative of all knowable reality. These traditional views surface in Max Stirner's "I" or ego, which shares with existentialism a tendency to absorb all of reality into itself, as if the universe turned on the choices of the self-oriented individual.*

More recent works on lifestyle anarchism generally sidestep Stirner's sovereign, all-encompassing "I," albeit retaining its egocentric emphasis, and tend toward existentialism, recycled Situationism, Buddhism, Taoism, antirationalism, and primitivism — or, quite ecumenically, all of them in various permutations. Their commonalities, as we shall see, are redolent of a prelapsarian return to an original, often diffuse, and even petulantly infantile ego that ostensibly precedes history, civilization, and a sophisticated technology — possibly language itself — and they have nourished more than one reactionary political ideology over the past century.

AUTONOMY OR FREEDOM?

WITHOUT FALLING INTO the trap of social constructionism that sees every category as a product of a given social order, we are obliged to ask for a definition of the "free individual." How does

---

*The philosophical pedigree of this ego and its fortunes can be traced through Fichte back to Kant. Stirner's view of the ego was merely a coarse mutation of the Kantian and particularly the Fichtean egos, marked by hectoring rather than insight.

individuality come into being, and under what circumstances is it free?

When lifestyle anarchists call for autonomy rather than freedom, they thereby forfeit the rich social connotations of freedom. Indeed, today's steady anarchist drumbeat for autonomy rather than social freedom cannot be dismissed as accidental, particularly in Anglo-American varieties of libertarian thought, where the notion of autonomy more closely corresponds to personal liberty. Its roots lie in the Roman imperial tradition of *libertas*, wherein the untrammeled ego is "free" to own his personal property — and to gratify his personal lusts. Today, the individual endowed with "sovereign rights" is seen by many lifestyle anarchists as antithetical not only to the State but to society as such.

Strictly defined, the Greek word *autonomia* means "independence," connoting a self-managing ego, independent of any clientage or reliance on others for its maintenance. To my knowledge, it was not widely used by the Greek philosophers; indeed, it is not even mentioned in F. E. Peters's historical lexicon of *Greek Philosophical Terms*. *Autonomy*, like *liberty*, refers to the man (or woman) who Plato would have ironically called the "master of himself," a condition "when the better principle of the human soul controls the worse." Even for Plato, the attempt to achieve autonomy through mastery of oneself constituted a paradox, "for the master is also the servant and the servant the master, and in all these modes of speaking the same person is predicated" (*Republic*, book 4, 431). Characteristically, Paul Goodman, an essentially individualistic anarchist, maintained that "for me, the chief principle of anarchism is not freedom but autonomy, the ability to initiate a task and do it one's own way" — a view worthy of an aesthete but not of a social revolutionary.[6]

While *autonomy* is associated with the presumably self-sovereign individual, *freedom* dialectically interweaves the individual with the collective. The word *freedom* has its analogue in the Greek *eleutheria* and derives from the German *Freiheit*, a term that still retains a *gemeinschäftliche* or communal ancestry in Teutonic tribal life and law. When applied to the individual, *freedom* thus preserves a social or collective interpretation of that individual's origins and development as a self. In "freedom," individual selfhood does not stand opposed to or apart from the collective but is significantly formed — and in a rational society, would be realized — by his or her own social existence. Freedom thus does not subsume the individual's liberty but denotes its actualization.*

The confusion between autonomy and freedom is all too evident in L. Susan Brown's *The Politics of Individualism (POI)*, a recent attempt to articulate and elaborate a basically individualist anarchism, yet retain some filiations with anarcho-communism.[7] If lifestyle anarchism needs an academic pedigree, it will find it in her attempt to meld Bakunin and Kropotkin with John Stuart Mill. Alas, herein lies a problem that is more than academic. Brown's work exhibits the extent to which concepts of personal autonomy stand at odds with concepts of social freedom. In essence, like Goodman she interprets anarchism as a philosophy not of social freedom but of personal autonomy. She then offers a notion of "existential individualism" that she contrasts sharply both with "instrumental individualism" (or C. B. Macpherson's "possessive [bourgeois] individualism") and with "collectivism" — leavened with extensive quotations from Emma Goldman, who was by no means the ablest thinker in the libertarian pantheon.

Brown's "existential individualism" shares liberalism's "commitment to individual autonomy and self-determination," she writes (*POI*, p. 2). "While much of anarchist theory has been viewed as communist by anarchists and non-anarchists alike," she observes, "what distinguishes anarchism from other communist philosophies is anarchism's uncompromising and relentless celebration of individual self-determination and autonomy. To be an anarchist — whether communist, individualist, mutualist, syndicalist, or feminist — is to affirm a commitment to the primacy of individual freedom" (*POI*, p. 2) — and

---

* Unfortunately, in Romance languages *freedom* is generally translated with a word derived from the Latin *libertas* — French *liberté*, Italian *libertà*, or Spanish *libertad*. English, which combines both German and Latin, allows for making a distinction between freedom and liberty, which other languages do not. I can only recommend that on this subject, writers in other languages use both English words as needed to retain the distinction between them.

here she uses the word *freedom* in the sense of autonomy. Although anarchism's "critique of private property and advocacy of free communal economic relations" (*POI*, p. 2) move Brown's anarchism beyond liberalism, it nonetheless upholds individual rights over — and *against* — those of the collective.

"What distinguishes [existential individualism] from the collectivist point of view," Brown goes on, "is that individualists" — anarchists no less than liberals — "believe in the existence of an internally motivated and authentic free will, while *most* collectivists understand the human individual as shaped externally by others — the individual for them is 'constructed' by the collective" (*POI*, p. 12, emphasis added). Essentially, Brown dismisses collectivism — not just state socialism, but collectivism as such — with the liberal canard that a collectivist society entails the subordination of the individual to the group. Her extraordinary suggestion that "*most* collectivists" have regarded individual people as "simply human flotsam and jetsam swept along in the current of history" (*POI*, p. 12) is a case in point. Stalin certainly held this view, and so did many Bolsheviks, with their hypostasization of social forces over individual desires and intentions. But collectivists *as such*? Are we to ignore the generous traditions of collectivism that sought a rational, democratic, and harmonious society — the visions of William Morris, say, or Gustav Landauer? What about Robert Owen, the Fourierists, democratic and libertarian socialists, Social Democrats of an earlier era, even Karl Marx and Peter Kropotkin? I am not sure that "*most* collectivists," even those who are anarchists, would accept the crude determinism that Brown attributes to Marx's social interpretations. By creating straw "collectivists" who are hard-line mechanists, Brown rhetorically counterposes a mysteriously and autogenetically constituted individual, on the one hand, with an omnipresent, presumably oppressive, even totalitarian collective, on the other. Brown, in effect, overstates the contrast between "existential individualism" and the beliefs of "most collectivists" — to the point where her arguments seem misguided at best or disingenuous at worst.

It is elementary that, Jean-Jacques Rousseau's ringing opening to the *Social Contract* notwithstanding, people are definitely *not* "born free," let alone autonomous. Indeed, quite to the contrary, they are born *very* unfree, highly dependent, and conspicuously heteronomous. What freedom, independence, and autonomy people have in a given historical period is the product of long social traditions and, yes, a *collective* development—which is not to deny that individuals play an important role in that development, indeed are ultimately obliged to do so if they wish to be free.*

Brown's argument leads to a surprisingly simplistic conclusion. "It is not the group that gives shape to the individual," we are told, "but rather individuals who give form and content to the group. A group is *a collection of individuals, no more and no less;* it has no life or consciousness of its own" (*POI*, p. 12, emphasis added). Not only does this incredible formulation closely resemble Margaret Thatcher's notorious statement that there is no such thing as a society but only individuals; it attests to a positivistic, indeed naive social myopia in which the universal is wholly separated from the concrete. Aristotle, one would have thought, resolved this problem when he chided Plato for creating a realm of ineffable "forms" that existed apart from their tangible and imperfect "copies."

It remains true that individuals never form mere "collections" — except perhaps in cyberspace; quite to the contrary, even when they seem atomized and hermetic, they are immensely defined by the relationships they establish or are obliged to establish with each other, by virtue of their very real existence as social beings. The idea that a collective — and by extrapolation, society — is merely a "collection of individuals, no more and no less" represents an "insight" into the nature of human

---

*In a delicious mockery of the myth that people are born free, Bakunin astutely declared: "How ridiculous are the ideas of the individualists of the Jean Jacques Rousseau school and of the Proudhonian mutualists who conceive society as the result of the free contract of individuals absolutely independent of one another and entering into mutual relations only because of the convention drawn up among men. As if these men had dropped from the skies, bringing with them speech, will, original thought, and as if they were alien to anything of the earth, that is, anything having social origin." Maximoff, *Political Philosophy of Bakunin*, p. 167.

consociation that is hardly liberal but, today particularly, potentially reactionary.

By insistently identifying collectivism with an implacable social determinism, Brown herself *creates* an abstract "individual," one that is not even existential in the strictly conventional sense of the word. Minimally, human existence *presupposes* the social and material conditions necessary for the maintenance of life, sanity, intelligence, and discourse; and the affective qualities Brown regards as essential for her voluntaristic form of communism: care, concern, and sharing. Lacking the rich articulation of social relationships in which people are embedded from birth through maturity to old age, a "collection of individuals" such as Brown posits would be, to put it bluntly, not a *society* at all. It would be literally a "collection" in Thatcher's sense of free-booting, self-seeking, egoistic monads. Presumably complete unto themselves, they are, by dialectical inversion, immensely *de*-individuated for want of any aim beyond the satisfaction of their own needs and pleasures — which are often socially engineered today in any case.

Acknowledging that individuals are self-motivated and possess free will does not require us to reject collectivism, given that they are also capable of developing an awareness of the social conditions under which these eminently human potentialities are exercised. The attainment of freedom rests partly on biological facts, as anyone who has raised a child knows; partly, on social facts, as anyone who lives in a community knows; and contrary to social constructionists, partly on the interaction of environment and inborn personal proclivities, as any thinking person knows. Individuality did not spring into being *ab novo*. Like the idea of freedom, it has a long social and psychological history.

Left to his or her own self, the individual loses the indispensable social moorings that make for what an anarchist might be expected to prize in individuality: reflective powers, which derive in great part from discourse; the emotional equipment that nourishes rage against unfreedom; the sociality that motivates the desire for radical change; and the sense of responsibility that engenders social action.

Indeed, Brown's thesis has disturbing implications for social action. If individual "autonomy" overrides any commitment to a "collectivity," there is no basis whatever for social institutionalization, decision-making, or even administrative coordination. Each individual, self-contained in his or her "autonomy," is free to do whatever he or she wants — presumably, following the old liberal formula, if it does not impede the "autonomy" of others. Even democratic decision-making is jettisoned as authoritarian. "Democratic rule is still rule," Brown warns. "While it allows for more individual participation in government than monarchy or totalitarian dictatorship, it still inherently involves the repression of the wills of some people. This is obviously at odds with the existential individual, who must maintain the integrity of will in order to *be* existentially free" (*POI*, p. 53). Indeed, so transcendentally sacrosanct is the autonomous individual will, in Brown's eyes, that she approvingly quotes Peter Marshall's claim that, according to anarchist principles, "the majority has no more right to dictate to the minority, *even a minority of one,* than the minority to the majority" (*POI*, p. 140, emphasis added).

Denigrating rational, discursive, and direct-democratic procedures for collective decision-making as "dictating" and "ruling" awards a minority of one sovereign ego the right to abort the decision of a majority. But the fact remains that a free society will either be democratic, or it will not be achieved at all. In the very *existential* situation, if you please, of an anarchist society — a direct libertarian democracy — decisions would most certainly be made following open discussion. Thereafter the outvoted minority — even a minority of one — would have every opportunity to present countervailing arguments to try to change that decision. Decision-making by consensus, on the other hand, precludes ongoing *dissensus* — the all-important process of continual dialogue, disagreement, challenge, and counter-challenge, without which social as well as individual creativity would be impossible.

If anything, functioning on the basis of consensus assures that important decision-making will be either manipulated by a minority or collapse completely. And the decisions that are made will embody the lowest common denominator of views and constitute the least creative level of agreement. I speak, here, from painful, years-long experience with the use of consensus in the Clamshell Alliance of the 1970s. Just at the moment when this quasi-anarchic antinuclear-power movement was at the peak of its struggle, with thousands of activists, it was destroyed through the manipulation of the consensus process by a minority. The "tyranny of structurelessness" that consensus decision-making produced permitted a well-organized few to control the unwieldy, deinstitutionalized, and largely disorganized many within the movement.

Nor, amidst the hue and cry for consensus, was it possible for *dissensus* to exist and creatively stimulate discussion, fostering a creative development of ideas that could yield new and ever-expanding perspectives. In any community, dissensus — and dissident individuals — prevent the community from stagnating. Pejorative words like *dictate* and *rule* properly refer to the silencing of dissenters, not to the exercise of democracy; ironically, it is the consensual "general will" that could well, in Rousseau's memorable phrase from the *Social Contract*, "force men to be free."

Far from being existential in any earthy sense of the word, Brown's "existential individualism" deals with the individual *ahistorically*. She rarefies the individual as a transcendental category, much as, in the 1970s, Robert K. Wolff paraded Kantian concepts of the individual in his dubious *Defense of Anarchism*. The social factors that interact with the individual to make him or her a truly willful and creative being are subsumed under transcendental moral abstractions that, given a purely intellectual life of their own, "exist" outside of history and praxis.

Alternating between moral transcendentalism and simplistic positivism in her approach to the individual's relationship with the collective, Brown's exposition fits together as clumsily as creationism with evolution. The rich dialectic and the ample history that shows how the individual was largely *formed by and interacted with* a social development is nearly absent from her work. Atomistic and narrowly analytic in many of her views, yet abstractly moral and even transcendental in her interpretations, Brown provides an excellent setting for a notion of autonomy that is antipodal to social freedom. With the "existential individual" on one side, and a society that consists of a "collection of individuals" and nothing more on the other, the chasm between autonomy and freedom becomes unbridgeable.*

ANARCHISM AS CHAOS

Whatever Brown's own preferences may be, her book both reflects and provides the premises for the shift among Euro-American anarchists away from social anarchism and toward individualist or lifestyle anarchism. Indeed, lifestyle anarchism today is finding its principal expression in spray-can graffiti, postmodernist nihilism, antirationalism, neoprimitivism, anti-technologism, neo-Situationist "cultural terrorism," mysticism, and a "practice" of staging Foucauldian "personal insurrections."

These trendy posturings, nearly all of which follow current yuppie fashions, are individualistic in the important sense that they are antithetical to the development of serious organizations, a radical politics, a committed social movement, theoretical coherence, and programmatic relevance. More oriented toward achieving one's own "self-realization" than achieving basic social change, this trend among lifestyle anarchists is

---

* Finally, Brown significantly misreads Bakunin, Kropotkin, and my own writings — a misreading that would require a detailed discussion to correct fully. For myself, I do not believe in a "'natural' human being," as Brown avers, any more than I share her archaic commitment to "natural law" (p. 159). "Natural law" may have been a useful concept during the era of democratic revolutions two centuries ago, but it is a philosophical myth whose moral premises have no more substance in reality than deep ecology's intuition of "intrinsic worth." Humanity's "second nature" (social evolution) has so vastly transformed "first nature" (biological evolution) that the word *natural* must be nuanced more carefully than Brown does. Her claim that I believe that "freedom is inherent to nature" grossly mistakes my distinction between a potentiality and its actualization (p. 160). To clarify my distinction between the potentiality for freedom in natural evolution and its still incomplete actualization in social evolution, the reader should consult my greatly revised *The Philosophy of Social Ecology: Essays in Dialectical Naturalism*, 2nd ed. (Montreal: Black Rose Books, 1995).

particularly noxious in that its "turning inward," as Katinka Matson called it, claims to be a politics — albeit one that resembles R. D. Laing's "politics of experience." The black flag, which revolutionary *social* anarchists raised in insurrectionary struggles in Ukraine and Spain, now becomes a fashionable sarong for the delectation of chic petty bourgeois.

One of the most unsavory examples of lifestyle anarchism is Hakim Bey's (aka Peter Lamborn Wilson's) *T.A.Z.: The Temporary Autonomous Zone, Ontological Anarchism, Poetic Terrorism*, a jewel in the New Autonomy Series (no accidental word choice here), published by the heavily postmodernist Semiotext(e)/Autonomedia group in Brooklyn.[8] Amid paeans to "Chaos," "Amour Fou," "Wild Children," "Paganism," "Art Sabotage," "Pirate Utopias," "Black Magic as Revolutionary Action," "Crime," and "Sorcery," not to speak of commendations of "Marxism-Stirnerism," the call for autonomy is taken to lengths so absurd as to seemingly parody a self-absorbed and self-absorbing ideology.

T.A.Z. presents itself as a state of mind, an ardently antirational and anticivilizational mood, in which disorganization is conceived as an art form and graffiti supplants programs. The Bey (his pseudonym is the Turkish word for "chief" or "prince") minces no words about his disdain for social revolution: "Why bother to confront a 'power' which has lost all meaning and become sheer Simulation? Such confrontations will only result in dangerous and ugly spasms of violence" (*TAZ*, p. 128). *Power* in quotation marks? A mere "Simulation"? If what is happening in Bosnia with firepower is a mere "simulation," we are living in a very safe and comfortable world indeed! The reader uneasy about the steadily multiplying social pathologies of modern life may be comforted by the Bey's Olympian thought that "realism demands not only that we give up *waiting* for 'the Revolution,' but also that we give up *wanting* it" (*TAZ*, p. 101). Does this passage beckon us to enjoy the serenity of Nirvana? Or a new Baudrillardian "Simulation"? Or perhaps a new Castoriadian "imaginary"?

Having eliminated the classical revolutionary aim of transforming society, the Bey patronizingly mocks those who once risked all for it: "The democrat, the socialist, the rational ideology . . . are deaf to the music & lack all sense of rhythm" (*TAZ*, p. 66).

Really? Have the Bey and his acolytes themselves mastered the verses and music of the *Marseillaise* and danced ecstatically to the rhythms of Gliere's *Russian Sailor's Dance*? There is a wearisome arrogance in the Bey's dismissal of the rich culture that was created by revolutionaries over the past centuries, indeed by ordinary working people in the pre-rock-'n'-roll, pre-Woodstock era.

Verily, let anyone who enters the dreamworld of the Bey give up all nonsense about social commitment. "A democratic dream? a socialist dream? Impossible," intones the Bey with overbearing certainty. "In dream we are never ruled except by love or sorcery" (*TAZ*, p. 64). Thus are the dreams of a new world evoked by centuries of idealists in great revolutions magisterially reduced by the Bey to the wisdom of his febrile dream world.

As to an anarchism that is "all cobwebby with Ethical Humanism, Free Thought, Muscular Atheism, & crude Fundamentalist Cartesian Logic" (*TAZ*, p. 52) — forget it! Not only does the Bey, with one fell swoop, dispose of the Enlightenment tradition in which anarchism, socialism, and the revolutionary movement were once rooted, he mixes apples like "Fundamentalist Cartesian Logic" with oranges like "Free Thought," and "Muscular Humanism" as though they were interchangeable or necessarily presuppose each other.

Although the Bey himself never hesitates to issue Olympian pronouncements and deliver petulant polemics, he has no patience with "the squabbling ideologues of anarchism & libertarianism" (*TAZ*, p. 46). Proclaiming that "Anarchy knows no dogmas" (*TAZ*, p. 52), the Bey nonetheless immerses his readers in a harsh dogma if there ever was one: "Anarchism ultimately implies anarchy — & anarchy is chaos" (*TAZ*, p. 64). So saith the Lord: "I *Am* That I Am" — and Moses quaked before the pronouncement!

Indeed, in a fit of manic narcissism, the Bey ordains that it is the all-possessive self, the towering "I," the Big "me" that is sovereign: "each of us [is] the ruler of our own flesh, our own creations — and as much of everything else as we can grab & hold." For the Bey, anarchists and kings — and beys — become indistinguishable, inasmuch as all are autarchs:

> Our actions are justified by fiat & our relations are shaped by treaties with other autarchs. We make the law

for our own domains — & the chains of law have been broken. At present perhaps we survive as mere Pretenders — but even so we may seize a few instants, a few square feet of reality over which to impose our absolute will, our *royaume. L'etat, c'est moi.* . . . If we are bound by any ethics or morality, it must be one which we ourselves have imagined. (*TAZ*, p. 67)

L'Etat, c'est moi? Along with beys, I can think of at least two people in this century who did enjoy these sweeping prerogatives: Joseph Stalin and Adolf Hitler. Most of the rest of us mortals, rich and poor alike, share, as Anatole France once put it, the prohibition to sleep under the bridges of the Seine. Indeed, if Friedrich Engels's "On Authority," with its defense of hierarchy, represents a bourgeois form of socialism, *T.A.Z.* and its offshoots represent a bourgeois form of anarchism. "There is no becoming," the Bey tells us, "no revolution, no struggle, no path; [if] already you're the monarch of your own skin — your inviolable freedom awaits to be completed only by the love of other monarchs: a politics of dream, urgent as the blueness of sky" — words that could be inscribed on the New York Stock Exchange as a credo for egotism and social indifference (*TAZ*, p. 4).

Certainly, this view will not repel the boutiques of capitalist "culture" any more than long hair, beards, and jeans have repelled the entrepreneurial world of haute fashion. Unfortunately, far too many people in this world — no "simulations" or "dreams" — do *not* own even their own skins, as prisoners in chain gangs and jails can attest in the most concrete of terms. No one has ever floated out of the earthly realm of misery on "a politics of dreams" except the privileged petty bourgeois, who may find the Bey's manifestoes amenable particularly in moments of boredom.

For the Bey, in fact, even classical revolutionary insurrections offer little more than a personal high, redolent of Foucault's "limit experiences." "An uprising is like a 'peak experience,'" he assures us (*TAZ*, p. 100). Historically, "some anarchists . . took part in all sorts of uprisings and revolutions, even communist & socialist ones," but that was "because they found in the moment of insurrection itself the kind of freedom they sought. Thus while utopianism has so far always failed, the individualist or existentialist anarchists have succeeded inasmuch as they have attained (however briefly) the realization of their will to power in war" (*TAZ*, p. 88). The Austrian workers' uprising of February 1934 and the Spanish Civil War of 1936, I can attest, were more than orgiastic "moments of insurrection" but were bitter struggles carried on with desperate earnestness and magnificent élan, all aesthetic epiphanies notwithstanding.

Insurrection nonetheless becomes for the Bey little more than a psychedelic "trip," while the Nietzschean Overman, of whom the Bey approves, is a "free spirit" who would "disdain wasting time on agitation for reform, on protest, on visionary dreams, on all kinds of 'revolutionary martyrdom.'" Presumably dreams are okay as long as they are not "visionary" (read: socially committed); rather, the Bey would "drink wine" and have a "private epiphany" (*TAZ*, p. 88), which suggests little more than mental masturbation, freed to be sure from the constraints of Cartesian logic.

It should not surprise us to learn that the Bey favors the ideas of Max Stirner, who "commits no metaphysics, yet bestows on the Unique [i.e, the Ego] a certain absoluteness" (*TAZ*, p. 68). To be sure, the Bey finds that there is a "missing ingredient in Stirner": "a working concept of *nonordinary consciousness*" (*TAZ*, p. 68). Apparently Stirner is too much the rationalist for the Bey. "The orient, the occult, the tribal cultures possess techniques which can be 'appropriated' in true anarchist fashion. . . . We need a practical kind of 'mystical anarchism' . . . a democratization of shamanism, intoxicated & serene" (*TAZ*, p. 63). Hence the Bey summons his disciples to become "sorcerers" and suggests that they use the "Black Malay Djinn Curse."

What, finally, is a "temporary autonomous zone"? "The TAZ is like an uprising which does not engage directly with the State, a guerrilla operation which liberates an area (of land, of time, of imagination) and then dissolves itself, to re-form elsewhere/elsewhen, *before* the State can crush it" (*TAZ*, p. 101). In a TAZ we can "realize many of our true Desires, even if only for a season, a brief Pirate Utopia, a warped free-zone in the old Space/Time continuum)" (*TAZ*, p. 62). "Potential TAZs" include "the sixties-style 'tribal gathering,' the forest conclave of eco-saboteurs, the idyllic Beltane of the neopagans, anarchist conferences, and gay faery circles," not to speak of "nightclubs, banquets," and "old-time libertarian picnics" — no less! (*TAZ*, p. 100). Having been a member of the Libertarian League in the 1960s, I would love to see the Bey and his disciples surface at an "old-time libertarian picnic"!

So transient, so evanescent, so ineffable is a TAZ in contrast to the formidably stable State and bourgeoisie that "as soon as the TAZ is named . . . it must vanish, it *will* vanish . . . only to spring up again somewhere else" (*TAZ*, p. 101). A TAZ, in effect, is not a revolt but precisely a simulation, an insurrection as lived in the imagination of a juvenile brain, a safe retreat into unreality. Indeed, declaims the Bey: "We recommend [the TAZ] because it can provide the quality of enhancement without necessarily [!] leading to violence & martyrdom" (*TAZ*, p. 101). More precisely, like an Andy Warhol "happening," a TAZ is a passing event, a momentary orgasm, a fleeting expression of the "will to power" that is, in fact, conspicuously powerless in its capacity to leave any imprint on the individual's personality, subjectivity, and even self-formation, still less on shaping events and reality.

Given the evanescent quality of a TAZ, the Bey's disciples can enjoy the fleeting privilege of living a "nomadic existence," for "homelessness can in a sense be a virtue, an adventure" (*TAZ*, p. 130). Alas, homelessness can be an "adventure" when one has a comfortable home to return to, while nomadism is the distinct luxury of those who can afford to live without earning their livelihood. Most of the "nomadic" hoboes I recall so vividly from the Great Depression era suffered desperate lives of hunger, disease, and indignity and usually died prematurely — as they still do, today, in the streets of urban America. The few gypsy-types who seemed to enjoy the "life of the road" were idiosyncratic at best and tragically neurotic at worst. Nor can I ignore another "insurrection" that the Bey advances: notably, "voluntary illiteracy" (*TAZ*, p. 129). Although he advances this as a revolt against the educational system, its more desirable effect might be to render the Bey's various ex cathedra injunctions inaccessible to his readers.

Perhaps no better description can be given of *T.A.Z.*'s message than the one that appeared in *Whole Earth Review*, whose reviewer emphasizes that the Bey's pamphlet is "quickly becom[ing] the countercultural bible of the 1990s... While many of Bey's concepts share an affinity with the doctrines of anarchism," the *Review* reassures its yuppie clientele that he

> pointedly departs from the usual *rhetoric* about overthrowing the government. Instead, he prefers the mercurial nature of "uprisings," which he believes provide "moments of intensity [that can] give shape and meaning to the entirety of life." These pockets of freedom, or temporary autonomous zones, enable the *individual* to elude the schematic grids of Big Government and to occasionally live within realms where he or she can *briefly* experience *total* freedom. (emphasis added)[9]

There is an untranslatable Yiddish word for all of this: *nebbich*! During the 1960s, the affinity group Up Against the Wall Motherfuckers spread similar confusion, disorganization, and "cultural terrorism," only to disappear from the political scene soon thereafter. Indeed, some of its members entered the commercial, professional, and middle-class world they had formerly professed to despise. Nor is such behavior uniquely American. As one French "veteran" of May-June 1968 cynically put it: "We had our fun in '68, and now it's time to grow up." The same deadening cycle, with circled A's, was repeated during a highly individualistic youth revolt in Zurich in 1984, only to end in the creation of Needle Park, a notorious cocaine and crack hangout established by the city's officials to allow addicted young people to destroy themselves legally.

The bourgeoisie has nothing whatever to fear from such lifestyle declamations. With its aversion for institutions, mass-based organizations, its largely subcultural orientation, its moral decadence, its celebration of transience, and its rejection of programs, this kind of narcissistic anarchism is socially innocuous, often merely a safety valve for discontent toward the prevailing social order. With the Bey, lifestyle anarchism takes flight from all meaningful social activism and a steadfast commitment to lasting and creative projects by dissolving itself into kicks, postmodernist nihilism, and a dizzying Nietzschean sense of elitist superiority.

The price that anarchism will pay if it permits this swill to displace the libertarian ideals of an earlier period could be enormous. The Bey's egocentric anarchism, with its postmodernist withdrawal into individualistic "autonomy," Foucauldian "limit experiences," and neo-Situationist "ecstasy," threatens to render the very word *anarchism* politically and socially harmless — a mere fad for the titillation of the petty bourgeois of all ages.

MYSTICAL AND IRRATIONALIST ANARCHISM

THE BEY'S *T.A.Z.* HARDLY stands alone in its appeal to sorcery, even mysticism. Given their prelapsarian mentality, many lifestyle anarchists readily take to antirationalism in its most atavistic forms. Consider "The Appeal of Anarchy," which occupies the entire back page of a recent issue of *Fifth Estate* (Summer 1989). "Anarchy," we read, recognizes "the *imminence* of *total liberation* [nothing less!] and as a sign of your freedom, be naked in your rites." Engage in "dancing, singing, laughing, feasting, playing," we are enjoined — and could anyone short of a mummified prig argue against these Rabelaisian delights?

But unfortunately, there is a hitch. Rabelais's Abbey of Thélème, which *Fifth Estate* seems to emulate, was replete with servants, cooks, grooms, and artisans, without whose hard labor the self-indulgent aristocrats of his distinctly upper-class utopia would have starved and huddled naked in the otherwise cold halls of the Abbey. To be sure, the *Fifth Estate*'s "Appeal of Anarchy" may well have in mind a materially simpler version of the Abbey of Thélème, and its "feasting" may refer more to tofu and rice than to stuffed partridges and tasty truffles. But *still* — without major technological advances to free people from toil, even to get tofu and rice on the table, how could a society based on this version of anarchy hope to "abolish all authority," "share all things in common," feast, and run naked, dancing and singing?

This question is particularly relevant for the *Fifth Estate* group. What is arresting in the periodical is the primitivistic, prerational, antitechnological, and anticivilizational cult that lies at the core of its articles. Thus *Fifth Estate*'s "Appeal" invites anarchists to "cast the magic circle, enter the trance of ecstasy, revel in sorcery which dispels all power" — precisely the magical techniques that shamans (who at least one of its writers celebrates) in tribal society, not to speak of priests in more developed societies, have used for ages to elevate their status as hierarchs and against which reason long had to battle to free the human mind from its own self-created mystifications. "Dispel *all* power"? Again, there is a touch of Foucault here that as always denies the need for establishing distinctly *empowered* self-managing institutions against the very real power of capitalist and hierarchical institutions — indeed, for the actualization of a society in which desire and ecstasy can find genuine fulfillment in a truly libertarian communism.

Fifth Estate's beguilingly "ecstatic" paean to "anarchy," so bereft of social content — all its rhetorical flourishes aside — could easily appear as a poster on the walls of a chic boutique, or on the back of a greeting card. Friends who recently visited New York City advise me, in fact, that a restaurant with linen-covered tables, fairly expensive menus, and a yuppie clientele on St. Mark's Place in the Lower East Side — a battleground of the 1960s — is named Anarchy. This feedlot for the city's petty bourgeoisie sports a print of the famous Italian mural *The Fourth Estate*, which shows insurrectionary fin de siècle workers militantly marching against an undepicted boss or possibly a police station. Lifestyle anarchism, it would seem, can easily become a choice consumer delicacy. The restaurant, I am told, also has security guards, presumably to keep out the local canaille who figure in the mural.

Safe, privatistic, hedonistic, and even cozy, lifestyle anarchism may easily provide the ready verbiage to spice up the pedestrian bourgeois lifeways of timid Rabelaisians. Like the "Situationist art" that MIT displayed for the delectation of the avant-garde petty bourgeoisie several years ago, it offers little more than a terribly "wicked" anarchist image — dare I say, a simulacrum — like those that flourish all along the Pacific Rim of America and points eastward. The Ecstasy Industry, for its part, is doing only too well under contemporary capitalism and could easily absorb the techniques of lifestyle anarchists to enhance a marketably naughty image. The counterculture that once shocked the petty bourgeoisie with its long hair, beards, dress, sexual freedom, and art has long since been upstaged by bourgeois entrepreneurs whose boutiques, cafés, clubs, and even nudist camps are doing a flourishing business, as witness the many steamy advertisements for new "ecstasies" in the *Village Voice* and similar periodicals.

Actually, *Fifth Estate*'s blatantly antirationalistic sentiments have very troubling implications. Its visceral celebration of imagination, ecstasy, and "primality" patently impugns not only rationalistic efficiency but reason as such. The cover of the Fall/Winter 1993 issue bears Francisco Goya's famously misunderstood *Capriccio* no. 43, *"Il sueno de la razon produce monstros"* ("The sleep of reason produces monsters"). Goya's sleeping figure is shown slumped over his desk before an Apple computer. *Fifth Estate*'s English translation of Goya's inscription reads, "The *dream* of reason produces monsters," implying that monsters are a product of reason itself. In point of fact, Goya avowedly meant, as his own notes indicate, that the monsters in the engraving are produced by the *sleep*, not the *dream*, of reason. As he wrote in his own commentary: "Imagination, deserted by reason, begets impossible monsters. United with reason, she is the mother of all arts, and the source of their wonders."[10] By deprecating reason, this on-again, off-again anarchist periodical enters into collusion with some of the most dismal aspects of today's neo-Heideggerian reaction.

AGAINST TECHNOLOGY AND CIVILIZATION

EVEN MORE TROUBLING are the writings of George Bradford (aka David Watson), one of the major theorists at *Fifth Estate,* on the horrors of technology — apparently technology *as such.* Technology, it would seem, determines social relations rather than the opposite, a notion that more closely approximates vulgar Marxism than, say, social ecology. "Technology is not an isolated project, or even an accumulation of technical knowledge," Bradford tells us in "Stopping the Industrial Hydra" (SIH),

> that is determined by a somehow separate and more fundamental sphere of "social relations." Mass technics have become, in the words of Langdon Winner, "structures whose conditions of operation demand the restructuring of their environments," and thus of the very social relations that brought them about. Mass technics — a product of earlier forms and archaic hierarchies —

have now outgrown the conditions that engendered them, taking on an autonomous life.... They furnish, or have become, a kind of total environment and social system, both in their general and individual, subjective aspects.... In such a mechanized pyramid ... instrumental and social relations are one and the same.[11]

This facile body of notions comfortably bypasses the capitalist relations that blatantly determine *how* technology will be used and focuses on what technology is presumed to *be*. By relegating social relations to something less than fundamental — instead of emphasizing the all-important productive process where technology is *used* — Bradford imparts to machines and "mass technics" a mystical autonomy that, like the Stalinist hypostasization of technology, has served extremely reactionary ends. The idea that technology has a life of its own is deeply rooted in the conservative German romanticism of the last century and in the writings of Martin Heidegger and Friedrich Georg Jünger, which fed into National Socialist ideology, however much the Nazis honored their antitechnological ideology in the breach.

Viewed in terms of the contemporary ideology of our own times, this ideological baggage is typified by the claim, so common today, that newly developed automated machinery variously costs people their jobs or intensifies their exploitation — both of which are indubitable facts but are anchored *precisely in social relations of capitalist exploitation*, not in technological advances per se. Stated bluntly: "downsizing" today is not being done by machines but by avaricious bourgeois who *use* machines to replace labor or exploit it more intensively.* Indeed, the very

---

* Displacing capitalism with the machine, thereby shifting the reader's attention from the all-important social relations that determine the use of technology to technology itself, appears in nearly the entire antitechnological literature of the past and present centuries. Jünger speaks for nearly all writers of this genre when he observes that "technical progress has constantly increased the total amount of work, and this is why unemployment spreads so far whenever crises and disturbances upset the organization of machine labor." See Friedrich Georg Jünger, *The Failure of Technology* (Chicago: Henry Regnery Company, 1956), p. 7.

machines that the bourgeois employs to reduce "labor costs" could, in a rational society, free human beings from mindless toil for more creative and personally rewarding activities.

There is no evidence that Bradford is familiar with Heidegger or Jünger; rather, he seems to draw his inspiration from Langdon Winner and Jacques Ellul, the latter of whom Bradford quotes approvingly: "It is the technological coherence that now makes up the social coherence. . . . Technology is in itself not only a means, but a universe of means — in the original sense of Universum: both exclusive and total" (quoted in *SIH*, p. 10).

In *The Technological Society*, his best-known book, Ellul advanced the dour thesis that the world and our ways of thinking about it are patterned on tools and machines *(la technique)*. Lacking any social explanation of how this "technological society" came about, Ellul's book concluded by offering no hope, still less any approach for redeeming humanity from its total absorption by *la technique*. Indeed, even a humanism that seeks to harness technology to meet human needs is reduced, in his view, into a "pious hope with no chance whatsoever of influencing technological evolution."[12] And rightly so, if so deterministic a worldview is followed to its logical conclusion.

Happily, however, Bradford provides us with a solution: "to begin immediately to dismantle the machine altogether" (*SIH*, p. 10). And he brooks no compromise with civilization but essentially repeats all the quasi-mystical, anticivilizational, and antitechnological clichés that appear in certain New Age environmental cults. Modern civilization, he tells us, is "a matrix of forces," including "commodity relations, mass communications, urbanization and mass technics, along with . . . interlocking, rival nuclear-cybernetic states," all of which converge into a "global megamachine" (*SIH*, p. 20). "Commodity relations," he notes in his essay "Civilization in Bulk" (*CIB*), are merely *part* of this "matrix of forces," in which civilization is "a machine" that has been a "labor camp from its origins," a "rigid pyramid of crusting hierarchies," "a grid expanding the territory of the inorganic," and "a linear progression from Prometheus' theft of fire to the International Monetary Fund."[13] Accordingly, Bradford reproves Monica Sjöo and Barbara Mor's inane book, *The Great Cosmic Mother: Rediscovering the Religion of the Earth* — not for its atavistic and regressive theism, but because the

SOCIAL ANARCHISM OR LIFESTYLE ANARCHISM

authors put the word *civilization* in quotation marks — a practice that "reflects the tendency of this fascinating [!] book to posit an alternative or reverse perspective on civilization rather than to challenge its terms altogether" (*CIB*, footnote 23). Presumably, it is Prometheus who is to be reproved, not these two Earth Mothers, whose tract on chthonic deities, for all its compromises with civilization, is "fascinating."

No reference to the megamachine would be complete, to be sure, without quoting from Lewis Mumford's lament on its social effects. Indeed, it is worth noting that such comments have normally misconstrued Mumford's intentions. Mumford was not an antitechnologist, as Bradford and others would have us believe; nor was he in any sense of the word a mystic who would have found Bradford's anticivilizational primitivism to his taste. On this score, I can speak from direct personal knowledge of Mumford's views, when we conversed at some length as participants in a conference at the University of Pennsylvania around 1972.

But one need only turn to his writings, such as *Technics and Civilization* (*TAC*), from which Bradford himself quotes, to see that Mumford is at pains to favorably describe "mechanical instruments" as "potentially a vehicle of rational human purposes."[14] Repeatedly reminding his reader that machines come from human beings, Mumford emphasizes that the machine is "the projection of one particular side of the human personality" (*TAC*, p. 317). Indeed, one of its most important functions has been to dispel the impact of superstition on the human mind. Thus:

> In the past, the irrational and demonic aspects of life had invaded spheres where they did not belong. It was a step in advance to discover that bacteria, not brownies, were responsible for curdling milk, and that an air-cooled motor was more effective than a witch's broomstick for rapid long distance transportation. . . . Science and technics stiffened our morale: by their very austerities and abnegations they . . . cast contempt on childish fears, childish guesses, equally childish assertions. (*TAC*, p. 324)

This major theme in Mumford's writings has been blatantly neglected by the primitivists in our midst—notably, his belief that the machine has made the "paramount contribution" of fostering "the technique of cooperative thought and action." Nor did Mumford hesitate to praise "the esthetic excellence of the machine form... above all, perhaps, the more objective personality that has come into existence through a more sensitive and understanding intercourse with these new social instruments and through their deliberate cultural assimilation" (*TAC*, p. 324). Indeed, "the technique of creating a neutral world of fact as distinguished from the raw data of immediate experience was the great general contribution of modern analytic science" (*TAC*, p. 361).

Far from sharing Bradford's explicit primitivism, Mumford sharply criticized those who reject the machine absolutely, and he regarded the "return to the absolute primitive" as a "neurotic adaptation" to the megamachine itself (*TAC*, p. 302), indeed a catastrophe. "More disastrous than any mere physical destruction of machines by the barbarian is his threat to turn off or divert the human motive power," he observed in the sharpest of terms, "discouraging the cooperative processes of thought and the disinterested research which are responsible for our major technical achievements" (*TAC*, p. 302). And he enjoined: "We must abandon our futile and lamentable dodges for resisting the machine by stultifying relapses into savagery" (*TAC*, p. 319).

Nor do his later works reveal any evidence that he relented in this view. Ironically, he contemptuously designated the Living Theater's performances and visions of the "Outlaw Territory" of motorcycle gangs as "Barbarism," and he deprecated Woodstock as the "Mass Mobilization of Youth," from which the "present mass-minded, over-regimented, depersonalized culture has nothing to fear."*

---

*Lewis Mumford, *The Pentagon of Power*, vol. 2 (New York: Harcourt Brace Jovanovich, 1970), captions to illustrations 13 and 26. This two-volume work has been consistently misread as an attack on technology, rationality, and science. In fact, as its prologue indicates, the work more properly counterposes the megamachine as a mode of organizing human labor — and, yes, social relations — to the achievements of science and technology, which Mumford normally celebrated and placed in the very social context that Bradford downplays.

Mumford, for his own part, favored neither the megamachine nor primitivism (the "organic") but rather the sophistication of technology along democratic and humanly scaled lines. "Our capacity to go *beyond* the machine [to a new synthesis] rests upon our power to *assimilate* the machine," he observed in *Technics and Civilization*. "Until we have *absorbed* the lessons of objectivity, impersonality, neutrality, the lessons of the mechanical realm, we cannot go further in our development toward the more richly organic, the more profoundly human" (*TAC*, p. 363, emphasis added).

Denouncing technology and civilization as inherently oppressive of humanity in fact serves to *veil* the specific social relations that privilege exploiters over the exploited and hierarchs over their subordinates. More than any oppressive society in the past, capitalism conceals its exploitation of humanity under a disguise of "fetishes," to use Marx's terminology in *Capital*, above all, the "fetishism of commodities," which has been variously — and superficially — embroidered by the Situationists into "spectacles" and by Baudrillard into "simulacra." Just as the bourgeoisie's acquisition of surplus value is hidden by a contractual exchange of wages for labor power that is only ostensibly equal, so the fetishization of the commodity and its movements conceals the sovereignty of capitalism's economic and social relations.

There is an important, indeed crucial, point to be made, here. Such concealment shields from public purview the causal role of capitalist competition in producing the crises of our times. To these mystifications, antitechnologists and anticivilizationists add the myth of technology and civilization as inherently oppressive, and they thus obscure the social relationships unique to capitalism — notably the use of things (commodities, exchange values, objects — employ what terms you choose) to mediate social relations and produce the techno-urban landscape of our time. Just as the substitution of the phrase "industrial society" for capitalism obscures the specific and primary role of capital and commodity relationships in forming modern society, so the substitution of a techno-urban culture for social relations, in which Bradford overtly engages, conceals the primary role of the market and competition in forming modern culture.

Lifestyle anarchism, largely because it is concerned with a "style" rather than a society, glosses over capitalist accumulation, with its roots in the competitive marketplace, as the source of ecological devastation, and gazes as if transfixed at the alleged break of humanity's "sacred" or "ecstatic" unity with "Nature" and at the "disenchantment of the world" by science, materialism, and "logocentricity."

Thus, instead of disclosing the sources of present-day social and personal pathologies, antitechnologism allows us to speciously replace capitalism with technology, which basically *facilitates* capital accumulation and the exploitation of labor, as the underlying cause of growth and of ecological destruction. Civilization, embodied in the city as a cultural center, is divested of its rational dimensions, as if the city were an unabated cancer rather than the potential sphere for universalizing human intercourse, in marked contrast to the parochial limitations of tribal and village life. The basic social relationships of capitalist exploitation and domination are overshadowed by metaphysical generalizations about the ego and *la technique*, blurring public insight into the basic causes of social and ecological crises — commodity relations that spawn the corporate brokers of power, industry, and wealth.

Which is not to deny that many technologies are inherently domineering and ecologically dangerous, or to assert that civilization has been an unmitigated blessing. Nuclear reactors, huge dams, highly centralized industrial complexes, the factory system, and the arms industry — like bureaucracy, urban blight, and contemporary media — have been pernicious almost from their inception. But the eighteenth and nineteenth centuries did not require the steam engine, mass manufacture, or, for that matter, giant cities and far-reaching bureaucracies, to deforest huge areas of North America and virtually obliterate its aboriginal peoples, or erode the soil of entire regions. To the contrary, even before railroads reached out to all parts of the land, much of this devastation had already been wrought using simple axes, black-powder muskets, horse-driven wagons, and moldboard plows.

It was these simple technologies that bourgeois enterprise — the barbarous dimensions of civilization of the last century —

used to carve much of the Ohio River valley into speculative real estate. In the South, plantation owners needed slave "hands" in great part because the machinery to plant and pick cotton did not exist; indeed, American tenant farming has disappeared over the past two generations largely because new machinery was introduced to replace the labor of "freed" black sharecroppers. In the nineteenth century peasants from semifeudal Europe, following river and canal routes, poured into the American wilderness and, with eminently unecological methods, began to produce the grains that eventually propelled American capitalism to economic hegemony in the world.

Bluntly put: it was capitalism — the *commodity* relationship expanded to its full historical proportions — that produced the explosive environmental crisis of modern times, beginning with early cottage-made commodities that were carried over the entire world in sailing vessels, powered by wind rather than engines. Apart from the textile villages and towns of Britain, where mass manufacture made its historic breakthrough, the machines that meet with the greatest opprobrium these days were created long *after* capitalism gained ascendancy in many parts of Europe and North America.

Despite the current swing of the pendulum from a glorification of European civilization to its wholesale denigration, however, we would do well to remember the significance of the rise of modern secularism, scientific knowledge, universalism, reason, and technologies that *potentially* offer the hope of a rational and emancipatory dispensation of social affairs, indeed, for the full realization of desire and ecstasy without the many servants and artisans who pandered to the appetites of their aristocratic "betters" in Rabelais's Abbey of Thélème. Ironically, the anti-civilizational anarchists who denounce civilization today are among those who enjoy its cultural fruits and make expansive, highly individualistic professions of liberty, with no sense of the painstaking developments in European history that made them possible. Kropotkin, for one, significantly emphasized "the progress of modern technics, which wonderfully simplifies the production of all the necessaries of life."[15] To those who lack a sense of historical contextuality, arrogant hindsight comes cheaply.

MYSTIFYING THE PRIMITIVE

THE COROLLARY OF antitechnologism and anticivilizationism is primitivism, an edenic glorification of prehistory and the desire to somehow return to its putative innocence.* Lifestyle anarchists like Bradford draw their inspiration from aboriginal peoples and myths of an edenic prehistory. Primal peoples, he says, "refused technology" — they "minimized the relative weight of instrumental or practical techniques and expanded the importance of . . . ecstatic techniques." This was because aboriginal peoples, with their animistic beliefs, were saturated by a "love" of animal life and wilderness — for them, "animals, plants, and natural objects" were *"persons,* even kin" (*CIB*, p. 11).

Accordingly, Bradford objects to the "official" view that designates the lifeways of prehistoric foraging cultures as "terrible,. brutish and nomadic, a bloody struggle for existence." Rather, he apotheosizes "the primal world" as what Marshall Sahlins called "the original affluent society,"

affluent because its needs are few, all its desires are easily met. Its tool kit is elegant and light-weight, its

---

* Anyone who advises us to significantly, even drastically, reduce our technology is also advising us, in all logic, to go back to the "stone age" — at least to the Neolithic or Paleolithic (early, middle, or late). In response to the argument that we cannot go back to the "primal world," Bradford attacks not the argument but those who make it: "Corporate engineers and leftist/syndicalist critics of capitalism" dismiss "any other perspective on technological domination . . . as 'regressive' and a 'technophobic' desire to go back to the stone age," he complains (*CIB*, footnote 3). I will leave aside the canard that favoring technological advance in itself implies favoring the extension of "domination," presumably of people and nonhuman nature. "Corporate engineers" and "leftist/syndicalist critics of capitalism" are by no means interchangeable in their outlook toward technology and its uses. In view of the fact that "leftist/syndicalist critics of capitalism" are laudably committed to serious class opposition to capitalism, their failures, today, to enlist a broad labor movement are more a tragedy to be mourned than an occasion for celebration.

> outlook linguistically complex and conceptually profound yet simple and accessible to all. Its culture is expansive and ecstatic. It is propertyless and communal, egalitarian and cooperative. . . . It is anarchic. . . . free of work . . . It is a dancing society, a singing society, a celebrating society, a dreaming society. (*CIB*, p. 10)

Inhabitants of the "primal world," according to Bradford, lived in harmony with the natural world and enjoyed all the benefits of affluence, including much leisure time. Primal society, he emphasizes, was "free of work" since hunting and gathering required much less effort than people today put in with the eight-hour day. He does compassionately concede that primal society was "capable of experiencing occasional hunger." This "hunger," however, was really symbolic and self-inflicted, you see, because primal peoples "sometimes [chose] hunger to enhance interrelatedness, to play, or to see visions" (*CIB*, p. 10).

It would take a full-sized essay in itself to unscramble, let alone refute, this absurd balderdash, in which a few truths are either mixed with or coated in sheer fantasy. Bradford bases his account, we are told, on "greater access to the views of primal people and their native descendants" by "a more critical . . . anthropology" (*CIB*, p. 10). In fact, much of his "critical anthropology" appears to derive from ideas propounded at the "Man the Hunter" symposium, convened in April 1966 at the University of Chicago.[16] Although most of the papers contributed to this symposium were immensely valuable, a number of them conformed to the naive mystification of "primitivity" that was percolating through the 1960s counterculture — and that lingers on to this day. The hippie culture, which influenced quite a few anthropologists of the time, averred that hunting-gathering peoples today had been bypassed by the social and economic forces at work in the rest of the world and still lived in a pristine state, as isolated remnants of Neolithic and Paleolithic lifeways. Further, as hunter-gatherers, their lives were notably healthy and peaceful, living then as now on an ample natural largess.

Thus, Richard B. Lee, coeditor of the collection of conference papers, estimated that the caloric intake of "primitive" peoples was quite high and their food supply abundant, making for a kind of virginal "affluence" in which people needed to forage only a few hours each day. "Life in the state of nature is not necessarily nasty, brutish, and short," wrote Lee. The habitat of the !Kung Bushmen of the Kalahari Desert, for example, "is abundant in naturally occurring foods." The Bushmen of the Dobe area, who, Lee wrote, were still on the verge of entry into the Neolithic,

> live well today on wild plants and meat, in spite of the fact that they are confined to the least productive portion of the range in which Bushmen peoples were formerly found. It is likely that an even more substantial subsistence base would have been characteristic of these hunters and gatherers in the past, when they had the pick of African habitats to choose from.[17]

Not quite! — as we shall see shortly.

It is all too common for those who swoon over "primal life" to lump together many millennia of prehistory, as if significantly different hominid and human species lived in one kind of social organization. The word *prehistory* is highly ambiguous. Inasmuch as the human genus included several different species, we can hardly equate the "outlook" of Aurignacian and Magdalenian foragers *(Homo sapiens sapiens)* some 30,000 years ago, with that of *Homo sapiens neanderthalensis* or *Homo erectus*, whose tool kits, artistic abilities, and capacities for speech were strikingly different.

Another concern is the extent to which prehistoric huntergatherers or foragers at various times lived in nonhierarchical societies. If the burials at Sungir (in present Eastern Europe) some 25,000 years ago allow for any speculation (and there are no Paleolithic people around to tell us about their lives), the extraordinarily rich collection of jewelry, lances, ivory spears, and beaded clothing at the gravesites of two adolescents suggest the existence of high-status family lines long before human beings settled down to food cultivation. Most cultures in the Paleolithic were probably relatively egalitarian, but hierarchy seems to have existed even in the late Paleolithic, with marked variations in degree, type, and scope of domination that cannot be subsumed under rhetorical paeans to Paleolithic egalitarianism.

A further concern that arises is the variation—in early cases, the absence — of communicative ability in different epochs. Inasmuch as a written language did not appear until well into historical times, the languages even of early *Homo sapiens sapiens* were hardly "conceptually profound." The pictographs, glyphs, and, above all, memorized material upon which "primal" peoples relied for knowledge of the past have obvious cultural limitations. Without a written literature that records the cumulative wisdom of generations, historical memory, let alone "conceptually profound" thoughts, are difficult to retain; rather, they are lost over time or woefully distorted. Least of all is orally transmitted history subject to demanding critique but instead easily becomes a tool for elite "seers" and shamans who, far from being "protopoets," as Bradford calls them, seem to have used their "knowledge" to serve their own social interests.[18]

Which brings us, inevitably, to John Zerzan, the anticivilizational primitivist par excellence. For Zerzan, one of the steady hands at *Anarchy: A Journal of Desire Armed*, the absence of speech, language, and writing is a positive boon. Another denizen of the "Man the Hunter" time warp, Zerzan maintains in his book *Future Primitive* (*FP*) that "life before domestication/agriculture was in fact largely one of a leisure, intimacy with nature, sensual wisdom, sexual equality, and health"[19] — with the difference that Zerzan's vision of "primality" more closely approximates four-legged animality. In fact, in Zerzanian paleoanthropology, the anatomical distinctions between *Homo sapiens*, on the one hand, and *Homo habilis, Homo erectus*, and the "much-maligned" Neanderthals, on the other, are dubious; all early *Homo* species, in his view, were possessed of the mental and physical capacities of *Homo sapiens* and furthermore lived in primal bliss for more than two million years.

If these hominids were as intelligent as modern humans, we may be naively tempted to ask, why did they not innovate technological change? "It strikes me as very plausible," Zerzan brightly conjectures, "that intelligence, informed by the success and satisfaction of a gatherer-hunter existence, is the very reason for the pronounced absence of 'progress.' Division of labor, domestication, symbolic culture — these were evidently [!] refused until very recently." The *Homo* species "long *chose* nature over culture," and by *culture* here Zerzan means "the manipulation of basic symbolic forms" (emphasis added) — an alienating encumbrance. Indeed, he continues, "reified time, language (written, certainly, and probably spoken language for all or most of this period), number, and art had no place, despite an intelligence fully capable of them" (*FP*, pp. 23, 24).

In short, hominids were capable of symbols, speech, and writing but deliberately rejected them, since they could understand one another and their environment instinctively, without recourse to them. Thus Zerzan eagerly agrees with an anthropologist who meditates that "San/Bushman communion with nature" reached "a level of experience that 'could almost be called mystical. For instance, they seemed to know what it actually felt like to be an elephant, a lion, an antelope'" even a baobab tree (*FP*, pp. 33-34).

The conscious "decision" to refuse language, sophisticated tools, temporality, and a division of labor (presumably they tried and grunted, "Bah!") was made, we are told, by *Homo habilis*, who, I should note, had roughly half the brain size of modern humans and probably lacked the anatomical capacity for syllabic speech. Yet we have it on Zerzan's sovereign authority that *habilis* (and possibly even *Australopithecus afarensis*, who may have been around some "two million years ago") possessed "an intelligence fully capable" — no less! — of these functions but refused to use them. In Zerzanian paleoanthropology, early hominids or humans could adopt or reject vital cultural traits like speech with sublime wisdom, the way monks take vows of silence.

But once the vow of silence was broken, *everything* went wrong! For reasons known only to God and Zerzan,

The emergence of symbolic culture, with its *inherent* will to manipulate and control, soon opened the door to the domestication of nature. After two million years of human life within the bounds of nature, in balance with other wild species, agriculture changed our lifestyle, our way of *adapting*, in an unprecedented way. Never before has such a radical change occurred in a species so utterly and so swiftly. . . . Self-domestication through language, ritual, and art *inspired* the taming of plants and animals that followed. (*FP*, pp. 27-28, emphasis added)

There is a certain splendor in this claptrap that is truly arresting. Significantly different epochs, hominid and/or human species, and ecological and technological situations are all swept up together into a shared life "within the bounds of nature." Zerzan's simplification of the highly complex dialectic between humans and nonhuman nature reveals a mentality so reductionist and simplistic that one is obliged to stand before it in awe.

To be sure, there is very much we can learn from preliterate cultures — organic societies, as I call them in *The Ecology of Freedom* — particularly about the mutability of what is commonly called "human nature." Their spirit of in-group cooperation and, in the best of cases, egalitarian outlook are not only admirable — and socially necessary in view of the precarious world in which they lived — but provide compelling evidence of the malleability of human behavior in contrast to the myth that competition and greed are innate human attributes. Indeed, their practices of usufruct and the inequality of equals are of great relevance to an ecological society.

But that "primal" or prehistoric peoples "revered" nonhuman nature is at best specious and at worst completely disingenuous. In the absence of "nonnatural" environments such as villages, towns, and cities, the very notion of "Nature" as distinguished from *habitat* had yet to be *conceptualized* — a truly alienating experience, in Zerzan's view. Nor is it likely that our remote ancestors viewed the natural world in a manner any less instrumental than did people in historical cultures. With due regard for their own material interests — their survival and well-being — prehistoric peoples seem to have hunted down as much game as they could, and if they imaginatively peopled the animal world with anthropomorphic attributes, as they surely did, it would have been to communicate with it with an end toward manipulating it, not simply toward revering it.

Thus, with very instrumental ends in mind, they conjured "talking" animals, animal "tribes" (often patterned on their own social structures), and responsive animal "spirits." Understandably, given their limited knowledge, they believed in the reality of dreams, where humans might fly and animals might talk — in an inexplicable, often frightening dream world that they took for reality. To control game animals, to use a habitat for survival purposes, to deal with the vicissitudes of weather and the like, prehistoric peoples had to *personify these phenomena and "talk" to them,* whether directly, ritualistically, or metaphorically.

In fact, prehistoric peoples seem to have intervened into their environment as resolutely as they could. As soon as *Homo erectus* or later human species learned to use fire, for example, they seem to have put it to work burning off forests, probably stampeding game animals over cliffs or into natural enclosures where they could be easily slaughtered. The "reverence for life" of prehistoric peoples thus reflected a highly pragmatic concern for enhancing and controlling the food supply, not a love for animals, forests, mountains (which they may very well have feared as the lofty home of deities both demonic and benign).[20]

Nor does the "love of nature" that Bradford attributes to "primal society" accurately depict foraging peoples today, who often deal rather harshly with work and game animals; the Ituri forest Pygmies, for example, tormented ensnared game quite sadistically, and Eskimos commonly maltreated their huskies.[21] As for Native Americans before European contact, they vastly altered much of the continent by using fire to clear lands for horticulture and for better visibility in hunting, to the extent that the "paradise" encountered by Europeans was "clearly humanized."[22]

Unavoidably, many Indian tribes seem to have exhausted local food animals and had to migrate to new territories to gain the material means of life. It would be surprising indeed if they did not engage in warfare to displace the original occupants. Their remote ancestors may well have pushed some of the great North American mammals of the last ice age (notably mammoths, mastodons, longhorn bison, horses, and camels) to extinction. Thickly accumulated bones of bison are still discernible in sites that suggest mass killings and "assembly-line" butchering in a number of American arroyos.[23]

Nor, among those peoples who did have agriculture, was land use necessarily ecologically benign. Around Lake Pátzcuaro in the central Mexican highlands, before the Spanish conquest, "prehistoric land use was not conservationist in practice," writes Karl W.

Butzer, but caused high rates of soil erosion. Indeed, aboriginal farming practices "could be as damaging as any pre-industrial land-use in the Old World."[24] Other studies have shown that forest overclearing and the failure of subsistence agriculture undermined Mayan society and contributed to its collapse.[25]

We will never have any way of knowing whether the lifeways of today's foraging cultures accurately mirror those of our ancestral past.* Not only did modern aboriginal cultures develop over thousands of years, but they were significantly altered by the diffusion of countless traits from other cultures before they were studied by Western researchers. Indeed, as

---

* It is odd to be told once again — this time by L. Susan Brown — that my "*evidence* of 'organic 'societies without any hierarchies at all is open to challenge" (emphasis added, p. 160). If Marjorie Cohen, whom Brown adduces, finds it "not convincing" to claim that "sexual symmetry and full equality" can be consistently demonstrated on the basis of existing "anthropological evidence" or that "the division of labour by sex" is not necessarily "compatible with sexual equality" — all I can say is: fine! They are not around to tell us, still less provide us with "convincing" evidence about anything. The same can be said about the gender relationships I suggested in *The Ecology of Freedom*. Indeed, all contemporary "anthropological evidence" regarding "sexual symmetry" is arguable because modern aborigines were conditioned for better or worse by European cultures long before modern anthropologists reached them.

What I tried to present in that book was a *dialectic* of gender equality and inequality, not a definitive account of prehistory — knowledge of which is necessarily lost to Brown, Cohen, and myself forever. I used modern data speculatively: to show that my conclusions are *reasonable*, which Brown flippantly dismisses in two sentences with no supportive data of any kind.

As for Brown's appeals to my lack of "evidence" on *how* hierarchy emerged, recent material on Mesoamerica, following the deciphering of the Mayan pictographs, bears out my reconstruction of the emergence of hierarchy. Finally, gerontocracy, whose priority I emphasize as probably the earliest form of hierarchy, is one of the most widespread hierarchical developments described in the anthropological literature.

Clifford Geertz has observed rather acidly, there is little if anything pristine about the aboriginal cultures that modern primitivists associate with early humanity. "The realization, grudging and belated, that [the pristine primality of existing aborigines] is not so, not even with the Pygmies, not even with the Eskimos," Geertz observes, "and that these people are in fact products of larger-scale processes of social change which have made them and continue to make them what they are — has come as something of a shock that has induced a virtual crisis in the field [of ethnography]."[26] Scores of "primal" peoples, like the forests they inhabited, were no more "virginal" at European contact than were the Lakota Indians at the time of the American Civil War, *Dancing With Wolves* to the contrary notwithstanding. Many of the much-touted "primal" belief-systems of existing aborigines are clearly traceable to Christian influences. Black Elk, for example, was a zealous Catholic,[27] while the late-nineteenth-century Ghost Dance of the Paiute and Lakota was profoundly influenced by Christian evangelical millennarianism.

In serious anthropological research, the notion of an "ecstatic," pristine hunter has not survived the thirty years that have passed since the "Man the Hunter" symposium. Most of the "affluent hunter" societies cited by devotees of the myth of "primitive affluence" literally devolved — probably very much against their desires — from horticultural social systems. The San people of the Kalahari are now known to have been gardeners before they were driven into the desert. Several hundred years ago, according to Edwin Wilmsen, San-speaking peoples were herding and farming, not to speak of trading with neighboring agricultural chiefdoms in a network that extended to the Indian Ocean. By the year 1000, excavations have shown, their area, Dobe, was populated by people who made ceramics, worked with iron, and herded cattle, exporting them to Europe by the 1840s together with massive amounts of ivory — much of it from elephants hunted by the San people themselves, who doubtless conducted this slaughter of their pachyderm "brothers" with the great sensitivity that Zerzan attributes to them. The marginal foraging lifeways of the San that so entranced observers in the 1960s were actually the result of economic changes in the late nineteenth century, while "the remoteness imagined by outside observers ... was not indigenous but was created by the collapse of mercantile capital."[28] Thus, "the current status of San-speaking peoples on the rural fringe of African economies," Wilmsen notes,

> can be accounted for only in terms of the social policies and economies of the colonial era and its aftermath. Their appearance as foragers is a function of their relegation to an underclass in the playing out of historical processes that began before the current millennium and culminated in the early decades of this century.[29]

The Yuquí of the Amazon, too, could easily have epitomized the pristine foraging society extolled in the 1960s. Unstudied by Europeans until the 1950s, this people had a tool kit that consisted of little more than a boar claw and bow-and-arrows: "In addition to being unable to produce fire," writes Allyn M. Stearman, who studied them, "they had no watercraft, no domestic animals (not even the dog), no stone, no ritual specialists, and only a rudimentary cosmology. They lived out their lives as nomads, wandering the forests of lowland Bolivia in search of game and other foods provided by their foraging skills."[30] They grew no crops at all and were unfamiliar with the use of the hook and line for fishing.

Yet far from being egalitarian, the Yuquí maintained the institution of hereditary slavery, dividing their society into a privileged elite stratum and a scorned laboring slave group. This feature is now regarded as a vestige of former horticultural lifeways. The Yuquí, it appears, were descended from a slaveholding pre-Columbian society, and "over time, they experienced deculturation, losing much of their cultural heritage as it became necessary to remain mobile and live off the land. But while many elements of their culture may have been lost, others were not. Slavery, evidently, was one of these."[31]

Not only has the myth of the "pristine" forager been shattered, but Richard Lee's own data on the caloric intake of "affluent" foragers have been significantly challenged by Wilmsen and his associates.[32] !Kung people had average lifespans of about thirty years. Infant mortality was high, and according to Wilmsen (*pace* Bradford!), the people were subject to disease and hunger during lean seasons. (Lee himself has revised his views on this score since the 1960s.)

Correspondingly, the lives of our early ancestors were most certainly anything but blissful. In fact, life for them was actually quite harsh, generally short, and materially very demanding. Anatomical assays of their longevity show that about half died in childhood or before the age of twenty, and few lived beyond their fiftieth year.* They were more likely scavengers than hunter-gatherers and were probably prey for leopards and hyenas.[33]

To members of their own bands, tribes, or clans, prehistoric and later foraging peoples were normally cooperative and peaceful; but toward members of other bands, tribes, or clans, they were often warlike, even sometimes genocidal in their efforts to dispossess them and appropriate their land. That most blissed-out of ancestral humans (if we are to believe the primitivists), *Homo erectus*, has left behind a bleak record of interhuman slaughter, according to data summarized by Paul Janssens.[34] It

---

*For the appalling statistics, see Corinne Shear Wood, *Human Sickness and Health: A Biocultural View* (Palo Alto, Calif.: Mayfield Publishing Co., 1979), pp. 17-23. Neanderthals — who far from being "maligned," as Zerzan would have it, are receiving a marvelous press these days — are very generously treated in Christopher Stringer and Clive Gamble's *In Search of the Neanderthals* (New York: Thames and Hudson, 1993). Yet these authors conclude: "The high incidence of degenerative joint disease in Neanderthals is perhaps not surprising given what we know of the hard lives they led and the wear and tear this would have produced on their bodies. But the prevalance of serious injuries is more surprising, and indicates just how dangerous life was, even for those who did not manage to reach 'old age' in Neanderthal societies" (pp. 94-95). Some prehistoric individuals no doubt lived into their seventies, such as the foragers who occupied the Florida marshes some eight thousand years ago, but these are very rare exceptions. But only a diehard primitivist would grasp at such exceptions and make them the rule. Oh, yes — conditions are terrible for most people under civilization. But who tries to claim that civilization is notable for unqualified joy, feasting, and love?

has been suggested that many individuals in China and Java were killed by volcanic eruptions, but the latter explanations loses a good deal of plausibility in the light of the remains of forty individuals whose mortally injured heads were decapitated — "hardly the action of a volcano," Corinne Shear Wood observes dryly.[35] As to modern foragers, the conflicts between Native American tribes are too numerous to cite at any great length — as witness the Anasazi and their neighbors in the Southwest, the tribes that were to finally make up the Iroquois Confederacy (the Confederacy itself was a matter of survival if they were not to all but exterminate one another), and the unrelenting conflict between Mohawks and Hurons, which led to the near extermination and flight of remanent Huron communities.

If the "desires" of prehistoric peoples "were easily met," as Bradford alleges, it was precisely because their material conditions of life — and hence their desires — were very simple indeed. Such might be expected of any life-form that largely *adapts* rather than *innovates*, that *conforms* to its pregiven habitat rather than *alters* it to make that habitat conform with its own wants. To be sure, early peoples had a marvelous understanding of the habitat in which they lived; they were, after all, highly intelligent and imaginative beings. Yet their "ecstatic" culture was unavoidably riddled not only by joy and "singing...celebrating...dreaming," but by superstition and easily manipulable fears.

Neither our remote ancestors nor existing aborigines could have survived if they held the "enchanted" Disneyland ideas imputed to them by present-day primitivists. Certainly, Europeans offered aboriginal peoples no magnificent social dispensation. Quite to the contrary: imperialists subjected native peoples to crass exploitation, outright genocide, diseases against which they had no immunity, and shameless plunder. No animistic conjurations did or could have prevented this onslaught, as at the tragedy of Wounded Knee in 1890, where the myth of ghost shirts impregnable to bullets was so painfully belied.

What is of crucial importance is that the regression to primitivism among lifestyle anarchists denies the most salient attributes of humanity as a species and the potentially emancipatory aspects of Euro-American civilization. Humans are vastly different from other animals in that they do more than merely *adapt* to the world around them; they *innovate* and create a new world, not only to discover their own powers as human beings but to make the world around them more suitable for their own development, both as individuals and as a species. Warped as this capacity is by the present irrational society, the ability to change the world is a natural endowment, the product of human biological evolution — not simply a product of technology, rationality, and civilization. That people who call themselves anarchists should advance a primitivism that verges on the animalistic, with its barely concealed message of adaptiveness and passivity, sullies centuries of revolutionary thought, ideals, and practice, indeed defames the memorable efforts of humanity to free itself from parochialism, mysticism, and superstition and change the world.

For lifestyle anarchists, particularly of the anticivilizational and primitivistic genre, history itself becomes a degrading monolith that swallows up all distinctions, mediations, phases of development, and social specificities. Capitalism and its contradictions are reduced to epiphenomena of an all-devouring civilization and its technological "imperatives" that lack nuance and differentiation. History, insofar as we conceive it as the unfolding of humanity's *rational* component — its *developing* potentiality for freedom, self-consciousness, and cooperation — is a complex account of the cultivation of human sensibilities, institutions, intellectuality, and knowledge, or what was once called "the education of humanity." To deal with history as a steady "Fall" from an animalistic "authenticity," as Zerzan, Bradford, and their compatriots do in varying degrees in a fashion very similar to that of Martin Heidegger, is to ignore the expanding ideals of freedom, individuality, and self-consciousness that have marked epochs of human development — not to speak of the widening scope of the revolutionary struggles to achieve these ends.

Anticivilizational lifestyle anarchism is merely one aspect of the social regression that marks the closing decades of the twentieth century. Just as capitalism threatens to unravel natural history by bringing it back to a simpler, less differentiated geological and zoological era, so anticivilizational lifestyle anarchism is complicit with capitalism in bringing the human spirit and its history back to a less developed, less determinate, pre-lapsarian world — the supposedly "innocent" pretechnological and precivilizatory society that existed before humanity's "fall from grace." Like the Lotus Eaters in Homer's *Odyssey*, humans are "authentic" when they live in an eternal present, without past or future — untroubled by memory or ideation, free of tradition, and unchallenged by becoming.

Ironically, the world idealized by primitivists would actually preclude the radical individualism celebrated by the individualist heirs of Max Stirner. Although contemporary "primal" communities have produced strongly etched individuals, the power of custom and the high degree of group solidarity impelled by demanding conditions allow little leeway for expansively individualistic behavior, of the kind demanded by Stirnerite anarchists who celebrate the supremacy of the ego. Today, dabbling in primitivism is precisely the privilege of affluent urbanites who can afford to toy with fantasies denied not only to the hungry and poor and to the "nomads" who by necessity inhabit urban streets but to the overworked employed. Modern working women with children could hardly do without washing machines to relieve them, however minimally, from their daily domestic labors — before going to work to earn what is often the greater part of their households' income. Ironically, even the collective that produces *Fifth Estate* found it could not do without a computer and was "forced" to purchase one — issuing the disingenuous disclaimer, "We hate it!"[36] Denouncing an advanced technology while using it to generate antitechnological literature is not only disingenuous but has sanctimonious dimensions: Such "hatred" of computers seems more like the belch of the privileged, who, having overstuffed themselves with delicacies, extol the virtues of poverty during Sunday prayers.

EVALUATING LIFESTYLE ANARCHISM

WHAT STANDS OUT most compellingly in today's lifestyle anarchism is its appetite for *immediacy* rather than reflection, for a naive one-to-one relationship between mind and reality. Not only does this immediacy immunize libertarian thinking from demands for nuanced and mediated reflection; it precludes rational analysis and, for that matter, rationality itself. Consigning humanity to the nontemporal, nonspatial, and nonhistorical —a "primal" notion of temporality based on the "eternal" cycles of "Nature" —it thereby divests mind of its creative uniqueness and its freedom to intervene into the natural world.

From the standpoint of primitivist lifestyle anarchism, human beings are at their best when they adapt to nonhuman nature rather than intervene in it, or when, disencumbered of reason, technology, civilization, and even speech, they live in placid "harmony" with existing reality, perhaps endowed with "natural rights," in a visceral and essentially mindless "ecstatic" condition. *T.A.Z., Fifth Estate, Anarchy: A Journal of Desire Armed*, and lumpen "zines" like Michael William's Stirnerite *Demolition Derby* — all focus on an unmediated, ahistorical, and anticivilizatory "primality" from which we have "fallen," a state of perfection and "authenticity" in which we were guided variously by the "bounds of nature," "natural law," or our devouring egos. History and civilization consist of nothing but a descent into the inauthenticity of "industrial society."

As I have already suggested, this mythos of a "falling from authenticity" has its roots in reactionary romanticism, most recently in the philosophy of Martin Heidegger, whose *völkisch* "spiritualism," latent in *Being and Time*, later emerged in his explicitly fascist works. This view now feeds on the quietistic mysticism that abounds in the antidemocratic writings of Rudolf Bahro, with its barely disguised appeal for "salvation" by a "Green Adolf," and in the apolitical quest for ecological spiritualism and "self-fulfillment" propounded by deep ecologists.

In the end, the individual ego becomes the supreme temple of reality, excluding history and becoming, democracy and responsibility. Indeed, lived contact with society as such is rendered tenuous by a narcissism so all-embracing that it shrivels consociation to an infantilized ego that is little more than a bundle of shrieking demands and claims for its own satisfactions. Civilization merely obstructs the ecstatic self-realization of this ego's desires, reified as the ultimate fulfillment of emancipation, as though ecstasy and desire were not products of cultivation and historical development, but merely innate impulses that appear ab novo in a desocialized world.

Like the petty-bourgeois Stirnerite ego, primitivist lifestyle anarchism allows no room for social institutions, political organizations, and radical programs, still less a public sphere, which all the writers we have examined automatically identify with statecraft. The sporadic, the unsystematic, the incoherent, the discontinuous, and the intuitive supplant the consistent, purposive, organized, and rational, indeed any form of sustained and focused activity apart from publishing a "zine" or pamphlet — or burning a garbage can. Imagination is counterposed to reason and desire to theoretical coherence, as though the two were in radical contradiction to each other. Goya's admonition that imagination without reason produces monsters is altered to leave the impression that imagination flourishes on an unmediated experience with an unnuanced "oneness." Thus is social nature essentially dissolved into biological nature; innovative humanity, into adaptive animality; temporality, into precivilizatory eternality; history, into an archaic cyclicity.

A bourgeois reality whose economic harshness grows starker and crasser with every passing day is shrewdly mutated by lifestyle anarchism into constellations of self-indulgence, inchoateness, indiscipline, and incoherence. In the 1960s, the Situationists, in the name of a "theory of the spectacle," in fact produced a reified spectacle of the theory, but they at least offered organizational correctives, such as workers' councils, that gave their aestheticism some ballast. Lifestyle anarchism, by assailing organization, programmatic commitment, and serious social analysis, apes the worst aspects of Situationist aestheticism without adhering to the project of building a movement. As the detritus of the 1960s, it wanders aimlessly within the bounds of the ego (renamed by Zerzan the "bounds of nature") and makes a virtue of bohemian incoherence.

What is most troubling is that the self-indulgent aesthetic vagaries of lifestyle anarchism significantly erode the socialist core of a left-libertarian ideology that once could claim social relevance and weight precisely for its uncompromising commitment to emancipation — not *outside* of history, in the realm of the subjective, but *within* history, in the realm of the objective. The great cry of the First International — which anarchosyndicalism and anarchocommunism retained after Marx and his supporters abandoned it — was the demand: "No rights without duties, no duties without rights." For generations, this slogan adorned the mastheads of what we must now retrospectively call *social* anarchist periodicals. Today, it stands radically at odds with the basically egocentric demand for "desire armed," and with Taoist contemplation and Buddhist nirvanas. Where social anarchism called upon people to rise in revolution and seek the reconstruction of *society*, the irate petty bourgeois who populate the subcultural world of lifestyle anarchism call for episodic rebellion and the satisfaction of their "desiring machines," to use the phraseology of Deleuze and Guattari.

The steady retreat from the historic commitment of classical anarchism to social struggle (without which self-realization and the fulfillment of desire in all its dimensions, not merely the instinctive, cannot be achieved) is inevitably accompanied by a disastrous mystification of experience and reality. The ego, identified almost fetishistically as the locus of emancipation, turns out to be identical to the "sovereign individual" of laissez-faire individualism. Detached from its social moorings, it achieves not autonomy but the heteronomous "selfhood" of petty-bourgeois enterprise.

Indeed, far from being free, the ego in its sovereign selfhood is bound hand and foot to the seemingly anonymous laws of the marketplace — the laws of competition and exploitation — which render the myth of individual freedom into another fetish concealing the implacable laws of capital accumulation. Lifestyle anarchism, in effect, turns out to be an additional mystifying bourgeois deception. Its acolytes are no more "autonomous" than the movements of the stock market, than price fluctuations and the mundane facts of bourgeois commerce. All claims to autonomy notwithstanding, this middle-class "rebel," with or without a brick in hand, *is entirely captive to the subterranean market forces that occupy all the allegedly "free" terrains of modern social life*, from food cooperatives to rural communes.

Capitalism swirls around us — not only materially but culturally. As John Zerzan so memorably put it to a puzzled interviewer who asked about the television set in the home of this foe of technology: "Like all other people, I have to be narcotized."[37]

That lifestyle anarchism itself is a "narcotizing" self-deception can best be seen in Max Stirner's *The Ego and His Own*, where the ego's claim to "uniqueness" in the temple of the sacrosanct "self" far outranks John Stuart Mill's liberal pieties. Indeed, with Stirner, egoism becomes a matter of epistemology. Cutting through the maze of contradictions and woefully incomplete statements that fill *The Ego and His Own,* one finds Stirner's "unique" ego to be a myth because its roots lie in its seeming "other" — society itself. Indeed: "Truth cannot step forward as you do," Stirner addresses the egoist, "cannot move, change, develop; truth awaits and recruits everything from *you,* and itself is only through you; for it exists only — *in your head.*"[38] The Stirnerite egoist, in effect, bids farewell to objective reality, to the facticity of the social, and thereby to fundamental social change and all ethical criteria and ideals beyond personal satisfaction amidst the hidden demons of the bourgeois marketplace. This absence of mediation subverts the very existence of the concrete, not to speak of the authority of the Stirnerite ego itself — a claim so all-encompassing as to exclude the social roots of the self and its formation in history.

Nietzsche, quite independently of Stirner, carried this view of truth to its logical conclusion by erasing the facticity and reality of truth as such: "What, then, is truth?" he asked. "A mobile army of metaphors, metonyms, and anthropomorphisms — in short, a sum of human relations, which have been enhanced, transposed, and embellished poetically and rhetorically."[39] With more forthrightness than Stirner, Nietzsche contended that facts are simply interpretations; indeed, he asked, "is it necessary to posit an interpreter behind the interpretations?" Apparently not, for "even this is invention, hypothesis."[40] Following Nietzsche's unrelenting logic, we are left with a self that not only essentially creates it own reality but also must justify its *own* existence as more than a mere interpretation. Such egoism thus annihilates the ego itself, which vanishes into the mist of Stirner's own unstated premises.

Similarly divested of history, society, and facticity beyond its own "metaphors," lifestyle anarchism lives in an asocial domain in which the ego, with its cryptic desires, must evaporate into logical abstractions. But reducing the ego to intuitive immediacy — anchoring it in mere animality, in the "bounds of nature," or in "natural law" — would amount to ignoring the fact that the ego is the product of an *ever-formative* history, indeed, a history that, if it is to consist of more than mere episodes, must avail itself of reason as a guide to standards of progress and regress, necessity and freedom, good and evil, and — yes! — civilization and barbarism. Indeed, an anarchism that seeks to avoid the shoals of sheer solipsism on the one hand and the loss of the "self" as a mere "interpretation" one the other must become explicitly socialist or collectivist. That is to say, it must be a *social* anarchism that seeks freedom through structure and mutual responsibility, not through a vaporous, nomadic ego that eschews the preconditions for social life.

Stated bluntly: Between the socialist pedigree of anarcho-syndicalism and anarchocommunism (which have never denied the importance of self-realization and the fulfillment of desire), and the basically liberal, individualistic pedigree of lifestyle anarchism (which fosters social ineffectuality, if not outright social negation), there exits a divide that cannot be bridged unless we completely disregard the profoundly different goals, methods, and underlying philosophy that distinguish them. Stirner's own project, in fact, emerged in a debate with the socialism of Wilhelm Weitling and Moses Hess, where he invoked egoism precisely to counterpose to socialism. "Personal insurrection rather than general revolution was [Stirner's] message," James J. Martin admiringly observes[41] — a counterposition that lives on today in lifestyle anarchism and its yuppie filiations, as distinguished from social anarchism with its roots in historicism, the social matrix of individuality, and its commitment to a rational society.

The very incongruity of these essentially mixed messages, which coexist on every page of the lifestyle "zines," reflects the feverish voice of the squirming petty bourgeois. If anarchism loses its socialist core and collectivist goal, if it drifts off into aestheticism, ecstasy, and desire, and, incongruously, into Taoist quietism and Buddhist self-effacement as a substitute for a libertarian program, politics, and organization, it will come to represent not social regeneration and a revolutionary vision but social decay and a petulant egoistic rebellion. Worse, it will feed the wave of mysticism that is already sweeping affluent members of the generation now in their teens and twenties. Lifestyle anarchism's exaltation of ecstasy, *certainly laudable in a radical social matrix* but here un-

SOCIAL ANARCHISM OR LIFESTYLE ANARCHISM

abashedly intermingled with "sorcery," is producing a dream-like absorption with spirits, ghosts, and Jungian archetypes rather than a rational and dialectical awareness of the world.

Characteristically, the cover of a recent issue of *Alternative Press Review* (Fall 1994), a widely read American feral anarchist periodical, is adorned with a three-headed Buddhist deity in serene nirvanic repose, against a presumably cosmic background of swirling galaxies and New Age paraphernalia — an image that could easily join *Fifth Estate*'s "Anarchy" poster in a New Age boutique. Inside the cover, a graphic cries out: "Life Can Be Magic When We Start to Break Free" (the A in *Magic* is circled) — to which one is obliged to ask: *How?* With *what?* The magazine itself contains a deep ecology essay by Glenn Parton (drawn from David Foreman's periodical *Wild Earth*) titled: "The Wild Self: Why I Am a Primitivist," extolling "primitive peoples" whose "way of life fits into the pre-given natural world," lamenting the Neolithic revolution, and identifying our "primary task" as being to "'unbuild' our civilization, and restore wilderness." The magazine's artwork celebrates vulgarity — human skulls and images of ruins are very much in evidence. Its lengthiest contribution, "Decadence," reprinted from *Black Eye*, melds the romantic with the lumpen, exultantly concluding: "It's time for a real Roman holiday, so bring on the barbarians!"

Alas, the barbarians are already here — and the "Roman holiday" in today's American cities flourishes on crack, thuggery, insensitivity, stupidity, primitivism, anticivilizationism, antirationalism, and a sizable dose of "anarchy" conceived as chaos. Lifestyle anarchism must be seen in the present social context not only of demoralized black ghettoes and reactionary white suburbs but even of Indian reservations, those ostensible centers of "primality," in which gangs of Indian youths now shoot at one another, drug dealing is rampant, and "gang graffiti greets visitors even at the sacred Window Rock monument," as Seth Mydans reports in *The New York Times* (March 3, 1995).

Thus, a widespread cultural decay has followed the degeneration of the 1960s New Left into postmodernism and of its counterculture into New Age spiritualism. For timid lifestyle anarchists, Halloween artwork and incendiary articles push hope and an understanding of reality into the ever-receding distance. Torn by the lures of "cultural terrorism" and Buddhist ashrams, lifestyle anarchists in fact find themselves in a crossfire between the barbarians at the top of society in Wall Street and the City, and those at its bottom, in the dismal urban ghettoes of Euro-America. Alas, the conflict in which they find themselves, for all their celebrations of lumpen lifeways (to which corporate barbarians are no strangers these days) has less to do with the need to create a free society than with a brutal war over who is to share in the in the available spoils from the sale of drugs, human bodies, exorbitant loans — and let us not forget junk bonds and international currencies.

A return to mere animality — or shall we call it "decivili-zation"? — *is a return not to freedom but to instinct*, to the domain of "authenticity" that is guided more by genes than by brains. Nothing could be further from the ideals of freedom spelled out in ever-expansive forms by the great revolutions of the past. And nothing could be more unrelenting in its sheer obedience to biochemical imperatives such as DNA or more in contrast to the creativity, ethics, and mutuality opened by culture and struggles for a rational civilization. There is no freedom in "wildness" if, by sheer ferality, we mean the dictates of inborn behavioral patterns that shape mere animality. To malign civilization without due recognition of its enormous potentialities for *self-conscious* free-dom — a freedom conferred by reason as well as emotion, by insight as well as desire, by prose as well as poetry — is to retreat back into the shadowy world of brutishness, when thought was dim and intellectuation was only an evolutionary promise.

Toward a Democratic Communalism

My picture of lifestyle anarchism is far from complete; the person-alistic thrust of this ideological clay allows it to be molded in many forms provided that words like *imagination, sacred, intui-tive, ecstasy,* and *primal* embellish its surface.

Social anarchism, in my view, is made of fundamentally different stuff, heir to the Enlightenment tradition, with due regard to that tradition's limits and incompleteness. Depending upon how it defines reason, social anarchism celebrates the thinking human mind without in any way denying passion, ecstasy, imagination, play, and art. Yet rather than reify them into hazy categories, it tries to incorporate them into everyday life. It is committed to rationality while opposing the rationalization of experience; to technology, while opposing the "megamachine"; to social institutionalization, while opposing class rule and hierarchy; to a genuine politics based on the confederal coordination of municipalities or communes by the people in direct face-to-face democracy, while opposing parliamentarism and the state.

This "Commune of communes," to use a traditional slogan of earlier revolutions, can be appropriately designated as Communalism. Opponents of democracy as "rule" to the contrary notwithstanding, it describes the *democratic* dimension of anarchism as a majoritarian administration of the public sphere. Accordingly, Communalism seeks freedom rather than autonomy in the sense that I have counterposed them. It sharply breaks with the psycho-personal Stirnerite, liberal, and bohemian ego as a self-contained sovereign by asserting that individuality does not emerge *ab novo*, dressed at birth in "natural rights," but sees individuality in great part as the ever-changing work of historical and social development, a process of self-formation that can be neither petrified by biologism nor arrested by temporally limited dogmas.

The sovereign, self-sufficient "individual" has always been a precarious basis upon which to anchor a left libertarian outlook. As Max Horkheimer once observed, "individuality is impaired when each man decides to fend for himself. . . . The absolutely isolated individual has always been an illusion. The most esteemed personal qualities, such as independence, will to freedom, sympathy, and the sense of justice, are social as well as individual virtues. The fully developed individual is the consummation of a fully developed society."[42]

If a left-libertarian vision of a future society is not to disappear in a bohemian and lumpen demimonde, it must offer a resolution to social problems, not flit arrogantly from slogan to slogan, shielding itself from rationality with bad poetry and vulgar graphics. Democracy is not antithetical to anarchism; nor are majority rule and nonconsensual decisions incommensurable with a libertarian society.

That no society can exist without institutional structures is transparently clear to anyone who has not been stupefied by Stirner and his kind. By denying institutions and democracy, lifestyle anarchism insulates itself from social reality, so that it can fume all the more with futile rage, thereby remaining a subcultural caper for gullible youth and bored consumers of black garments and ecstasy posters. To argue that democracy and anarchism are incompatible because any impediment to the wishes of even "a minority of one" constitutes a violation of personal autonomy is to advocate not a free society but Brown's "collection of individuals" — in short, a herd. No longer would "imagination" come to "power." Power, *which always exists,* will belong either to the collective in a face-to-face and clearly institutionalized democracy, or to the egos of a few oligarchs who will produce a "tyranny of structurelessness."

Not unjustifiably, Kropotkin, in his *Encyclopaedia Britannica* article, regarded the Stirnerite ego as elitist and deprecated it as hierarchical. Approvingly, he cited V. Basch's criticism of Stirner's individual anarchism as a form of elitism, maintaining "that the aim of all superior civilization is, not to permit *all* members of the community to develop in a normal way, but to permit certain better endowed individuals 'fully to develop,' even at the cost of the happiness and the very existence of the mass of mankind." In anarchism, this produces, in effect, a regression

> toward the most common individualism, advocated by all the would-be superior minorities to which indeed man owes in his history precisely the State and the rest, which these individualists combat. Their individualism goes so far as to end in a negation of their own starting-point — to say nothing of the impossibility of the individual to attain a really full development in the conditions of oppression of the masses by the "beautiful aristocracies."[43]

In its amoralism, this elitism easily lends itself to the unfreedom of the "masses" by ultimately placing them in the custody of the "unique ones," a logic that may yield a leadership principle characteristic of fascist ideology.[44]

In the United States and much of Europe, precisely at a time when mass disillusionment with the state has reached unprecedented proportions, anarchism is in retreat. Dissatisfaction with government as such runs high on both sides of the Atlantic—and seldom in recent memory has there been a more compelling popular sentiment for a new politics, even a new social dispensation that can give to people a sense of direction that allows for security and ethical meaning. If the failure of anarchism to address this situation can be attributed to any single source, the insularity of lifestyle anarchism and its individualistic underpinnings must be singled out for aborting the entry of a potential left-libertarian movement into an ever-contracting public sphere.

To its credit, anarchosyndicalism in its heyday tried to engage in a living practice and create an organized movement—so alien to lifestyle anarchism—within the working class. Its major problems lay not in its desire for structure and involvement, for program and social mobilization, but in the waning of the working class as a revolutionary subject, particularly after the Spanish Revolution. To say that anarchism lacked a politics, however, conceived in its original Greek meaning as the self-management of the community—the historic "Commune of communes"—is to repudiate a historic and *transformative* practice that seeks to radicalize the democracy inherent in any republic and to create a municipalist confederal power to countervail the state.*

---

*In his repellent "review" of my book *The Rise of Urbanization and the Decline of Citizenship* (since retitled *Urbanization Without Cities*), John Zerzan repeats the canard that classical Athens has "long been Bookchin's model for a revitalization of urban politics." In fact, I took great pains to indicate the failings of the Athenian *polis* (slavery, patriarchy, class antagonisms, and war). My slogan "Democratize the republic, radicalize the democracy" that lies latent in the republic — with the explicit aim of creating a dual power — is cynically truncated to read: "We must, [Bookchin] counsels, slowly enlarge and expand the 'existing institutions' and 'try to democratize the republic.'" This deceptive manipulation of ideas earns praise from Lev Chernyi (aka Jason McQuinn), of *Anarchy: A Journal of Desire Armed* and *Alternative Press Review*, in his hortatory preface to Zerzan's *Future Primitive* (see pp. 11, 164, 165).

The most creative feature of traditional anarchism is its commitment to four basic tenets: a confederation of decentralized municipalities; an unwavering opposition to statism; a belief in direct democracy; and a vision of a libertarian communist society. The most important issue that left-libertarianism — libertarian socialism no less than anarchism — faces today is: What will it *do* with these four powerful tenets? How will we give them social *form* and *content*? In what *ways* and by what *means* will we render them relevant to our time and bring them to the service of an organized popular movement for empowerment and freedom?

Anarchism must not be dissipated in self-indulgent behavior like that of the primitivistic Adamites of the sixteenth century, who "wandered through the woods naked, singing and dancing," as Kenneth Rexroth contemptuously observed, spending "their time in a continuous sexual orgy" until they were hunted down by Jan Zizka and exterminated — much to the relief of a disgusted peasantry, whose lands they had plundered.[45] It must not retreat into the primitivistic demimonde of the John Zerzans and George Bradfords. I would be the last to contend that anarchists should not live their anarchism as much as possible on a day-to-day basis — personally as well as socially, aesthetically as well as pragmatically. But they should not live an anarchism that diminishes, indeed effaces the most important features that have distinguished anarchism, as a movement, practice, and program, from statist socialism. Anarchism today must resolutely retain its character as a *social* movement — a *programmatic* as well as activist social movement — a movement that melds its embattled vision of a libertarian communist society with its forthright critique of capitalism, unobscured by names like "industrial society."

In short, social anarchism must resolutely affirm its differences with lifestyle anarchism. If a social anarchist movement cannot translate its fourfold tenets — municipal confederalism, opposition to statism, direct democracy, and ultimately libertarian communism — into a lived practice in a new public sphere; if these tenets languish like its memories of past struggles in ceremonial pronouncements and meetings; worse still, if they are subverted by the "libertarian" Ecstasy Industry and by quietistic Asian theisms, then its revolutionary socialistic core will have to be restored under a new name.

Certainly, it is already no longer possible, in my view, to call oneself an anarchist without adding a qualifying adjective to distinguish oneself from lifestyle anarchists. Minimally, social anarchism is radically at odds with anarchism focused on lifestyle, neo-Situationist paeans to ecstasy, and the sovereignty of the ever-shriveling petty-bourgeois ego. The two diverge completely in their defining principles — socialism or individualism. Between a committed revolutionary body of ideas and practice, on the one hand, and a vagrant yearning for privatistic ecstasy and self-realization on the other, there can be no commonality. Mere opposition to the state may well unite fascistic lumpens with Stirnerite lumpens, a phenomenon that is not without its historical precedents.

— June 1, 1995

Notes

I would like to thank my colleague and companion, Janet Biehl, for her invaluable assistance in researching material for and editing this essay.

1. *The Political Philosophy of Bakunin*, G. P. Maximoff editor (Glencoe, Ill.: Free Press, 1953), p. 144.
2. *Political Philosophy of Bakunin*, p. 158.
3. Peter Kropotkin, "Anarchism," the *Encyclopaedia Britannica* article, in *Kropotkin's Revolutionary Pamphlets*, ed. Roger N. Baldwin (New York: Dover Publications, 1970), pp. 285-87.
4. Katinka Matson, "Preface," *The Psychology Today Omnibook of Personal Development* (New York: William Morrow & Co., 1977), n.p.
5. Michel Foucault, *The History of Sexuality*, vol. 1, translated by Robert Hurley (New York: Vintage Books, 1990), pp. 95-96. Heavenly will be the day when one can get straightforward formulations from Foucault, interpretations of whose views are often contradictory.
6. Paul Goodman, "Politics Within Limits," in *Crazy Hope and Finite Experience: Final Essays of Paul Goodman*, ed. Taylor Stoehr (San Francisco: Jossey-Bass, 1994), p. 56.

7. L. Susan Brown, *The Politics of Individualism* (Montreal: Black Rose Books, 1993). Brown's hazy commitment to anarchocommunism seems to derive more from a visceral preference than from her analysis.

8. Hakim Bey, *T.A.Z.: The Temporary Autonomous Zone, Ontological Anarchism, Poetic Terrorism* (Brooklyn, NY: Autonomedia, 1985, 1991). Bey's individualism might easily resemble that of the late Fredy Perlman and his anticivilizational acolytes and primitivists in Detroit's *Fifth Estate*, except that *T.A.Z.* rather confusedly calls for "a *psychic paleolithism* based on High-Tech" (p. 44).

9. "T.A.Z.," *The Whole Earth Review* (Spring 1994), p. 61.

10. Cited by Jose Lopez-Rey, *Goya's Capriccios: Beauty, Reason and Caricature,* vol. 1 (Princeton, N.J.: Princeton University Press, 1953), pp. 80-81.

11. George Bradford, "Stopping the Industrial Hydra: Revolution Against the Megamachine," *The Fifth Estate*, vol. 24, no. 3 (Winter 1990), p. 10.

12. Jacques Ellul, *The Technological Society* (New York: Vintage Books, 1964), p. 430.

13. Bradford, "Civilization in Bulk, *Fifth Estate* (Spring 1991), p. 12.

14. Lewis Mumford, *Technics and Civilization* (New York and Burlingame: Harcourt Brace & World, 1963), p. 301. All page numbers herein refer to this edition.

15. Kropotkin, "Anarchism," *Revolutionary Pamphlets*, p. 285.

16. The conference papers were published in Richard B. Lee and Irven DeVore, eds., *Man the Hunter* (Chicago: Aldine Publishing Co., 1968).

17. "What Hunters Do for a Living, or, How to Make Out in Scarce Resources," in Lee and Devore, *Man the Hunter*, p. 43.

18. See particularly Paul Radin's *The World of Primitive Man* (New York: Grove Press, 1953), pp. 139-150.

19. John Zerzan, *Future Primitive and Other Essays* (Brooklyn, NY: Autonomedia, 1994), p. 16. The reader who has faith in Zerzan's research may try looking for important sources like "Cohen (1974)" and "Clark (1979)" (cited on pages 24 and 29, respectively) in his bibliography — they and others are entirely absent.

20. The literature on these aspects of prehistoric life is very large. Anthony Legge and Peter A. Rowly's "Gazelle Killing in Stone Age Syria," *Scientific American,* vol. 257 (Aug. 1987), pp. 88-95, shows

that migrating animals could have been slaughtered with devastating effectiveness by the use of corrals. The classical study of the pragmatic aspects of animism is Bronislaw Malinowski's *Myth, Science and Religion* (Garden City, N.Y.: Doubleday, 1954). Manipulative anthropomorphization is evident in many accounts of transmigrations from the human to nonhuman realm claimed by shamans, as in the myths of the Makuna reported by Kaj Århem, "Dance of the Water People," *Natural History* (Jan. 1992).

21. On the pygmies, see Colin M. Turnbull, *The Forest People: A Study of the Pygmies of the Congo* (New York: Clarion/Simon and Schuster, 1961), pp. 101-102. On the Eskimos, see Gontran de Montaigne Poncins's *Kabloona: A White Man in the Arctic Among the Eskimos* (New York: Reynal & Hitchcock, 1941), pp. 208-9, as well as in many other works on traditional Eskimo culture.

22. That many grasslands throughout the world were produced by fire, probably dating back to *Homo erectus*, is a hypothesis scattered throughout the anthropological literature. An excellent study is Stephen J. Pyne's *Fire in America* (Princeton, N.J.: Princeton University Press, 1982). See also William M. Denevan, in *Annals of the American Association of Geographers* (Sept. 1992), cited in William K. Stevens, "An Eden in Ancient America? Not Really," *The New York Times* (March 30, 1993), p. C1.

23. On the hotly debated issue of "overkill" see *Pleistocene Extinctions: The Search for a Cause*, ed. P. S. Martin and H. E. Wright, Jr. . The arguments around whether climatic factors and/or human "overkilling" led to massive extinctions of some thirty-five genera of Pleistocene mammals are too complex to be dealt with here. See Paul S. Martin, "Prehistoric Overkill," in *Pleistocene Extinctions: The Search for a Cause*, ed. P. S. Martin and H. E. Wright, Jr. (New Haven: Yale University Press, 1967). I have explored some of the arguments in my introduction to the 1991 revised edition of *The Ecology of Freedom* (Montreal: Black Rose Books). The evidence is still under debate. Mastodons, who were once regarded as environmentally restricted animals, are now known to have been ecologically more flexible and might have been killed off by Paleoindian hunters, possibly with far less compunction than romantic environmentalists would like to believe. I do not contend that hunting alone pushed these large mammals to extermination — a considerable amount of killing would have been enough.

A summary of arroyo drives of bison can be found in Brian Fagan, "Bison Hunters of the Northern Plains," *Archaeology* (May-June 1994), p. 38.

24. Karl W. Butzer, "No Eden in the New World," *Nature*, vol. 82 (March 4, 1993), pp. 15-17.

25. T. Patrick Cuthbert, "The Collapse of Classic Maya Civilization," in *The Collapse of Ancient States and Civilizations*, ed. Norman Yoffee and George L. Cowgill (Tucson, Ariz.: University of Arizona Press, 1988); and Joseph A. Tainter, *The Collapse of Complex Societies* (Cambridge: Cambridge University Press, 1988), esp. chapter 5.

26. Clifford Geertz, "Life on the Edge," *The New York Review of Books*, April 7, 1994, p. 3.

27. As William Powers observes, the book "*Black Elk Speaks* was published in 1932. There is no trace of Black Elk's Christian life in it." For a thorough debunking of the current fascination with the Black Elk story, see William Powers, "When Black Elk Speaks, Everybody Listens," *Social Text*, vol. 8, no. 2 (1991), pp. 43-56.

28. Edwin N. Wilmsen, *Land Filled With Flies* (Chicago: University of Chicago Press, 1989), p. 127.

29. Wilmsen, *Land Filled with Flies*, p. 3.

30. Allyn Maclean Stearman, *Yuquí: Forest Nomads in a Changing World* (Fort Worth and Chicago: Holt, Rinehart and Winston, 1989), p. 23.

31. Stearman, *Yuquí*, pp. 80-81.

32. Wilmsen, *Land Filled with Flies*, pp. 235-39 and 303-15.

33. See, for example, Robert J. Blumenschine and John A. Cavallo, "Scavenging and Human Evolution," *Scientific American* (October 1992), pp. 90-96.

34. Paul A. Janssens, *Paleopathology: Diseases and Injuries of Prehistoric Man* (London: John Baker, 1970).

35. Wood, *Human Sickness*, p. 20.

36. E. B. Maple, "The Fifth Estate Enters the 20th Century. We Get a Computer and Hate It!" *The Fifth Estate*, vol. 28, no. 2 (Summer 1993), pp. 6-7.

37. Quoted in *The New York Times*, May 7, 1995. Less sanctimonious people than Zerzan have tried to escape the hold of television and take their pleasures with decent music, radio plays, books, and the like. They just don't buy them!

38. Max Stirner, *The Ego and His Own*, ed. James J. Martin, trans. Steven T. Byington (New York: Libertarian Book Club, 1963), part 2,

chap. 4, sec. C, "My Self-Engagement," p. 352, emphasis added.

39. Friedrich Nietzsche, "On Truth and Lie in an Extra-Moral Sense" (1873; fragment), in *The Portable Nietzsche*, edited and translated by Walter Kaufmann (New York: Viking Portable Library, 1959), pp. 46-47.

40. Friedrich Nietzsche, fragment 481 (1883-1888), *The Will to Power*, trans. Walter Kaufmann and R. J. Hollingdale (New York: Random House, 1967), p. 267.

41. James J. Martin, editor's introduction to Stirner, *Ego and His Own*, p. xviii.

42. Max Horkheimer, *The Eclipse of Reason* (New York: Oxford University Press, 1947), p. 135.

43. Kropotkin, "Anarchism," *Revolutionary Pamphlets*, pp. 287, 293.

44. Kropotkin, "Anarchism," *Revolutionary Pamphlets*, pp. 292-93.

45. Kenneth Rexroth, *Communalism* (New York: Seabury Press, 1974), p. 89.

THE LEFT THAT WAS:
A PERSONAL REFLECTION

I would like to recall a Left That Was — an idealistic, often theoretically coherent Left that militantly emphasized its internationalism, its rationality in its treatment of reality, its democratic spirit, and its vigorous revolutionary aspirations. From a retrospective viewpoint of a hundred years or so, it is easy to find many failings in the Left That Was: I have spent much of my own life criticizing the Left's failings (as I saw them) and many of its premises, such as its emphasis on the historical primacy of economic factors (although this fault can be overstated by ignoring its social idealism), its fixation on the proletariat as a "hegemonic" class, and its failure to understand the problems raised by status hierarchy and domination.

But the Left That Was — the Left of the nineteenth and early twentieth century — did not have our devastating experiences with Bolshevism and particularly Stalinism to correct its weaknesses. It developed in a time of a rising mass movement of working people — a proletariat, in particular — that had not gained anything from the democratic revolutions of the past (as had the peasantry). The Left That Was, nonetheless, had features that should be regarded as imperishable for *any* movement that seeks to create a better world — a rich generosity of spirit, a commitment to a humane world, a rare degree of political independence, a vibrant revolutionary spirit, and an unwavering opposition to capitalism. These attributes were characteristics of the Left That Was, by which I mean not the Leninist "Old Left" or the Maoist "New Left" that followed, but traditional ideas underlying the Left as such. They *defined* the Left and distinguished it from liberalism, progressivism, reformism, and the like.

My concern, here, is that these attributes are fading rapidly from the present-day Left. The Left today has withdrawn into a strident form of nationalism and statism, presumably in the interests of "national liberation"; an inchoate nihilism, presumably under the aegis of postmodernism; and an ethnic parochialism, presumably in the name of fighting racial discrimination. New versions of nationalism, a lack of concern for democracy, and a fragmenting sectorialism and parochialism abound. Dogmatism and moral intimidation have turned this sectorialism and parochialism into a whiplash, one that silences all analyses that go beyond mere bumper-sticker slogans.

Too many careers and reputations are being made by many "leaders" in the present-day Left through shrill voices rather than clear insights. Their sloganeering has no content, and their verbiage offers little understanding of the fact that we are all ultimately one community of human beings, and that we can transcend the mere conditioned reflexes that undermine our commitment to mutual recognition and care for each other as well as the planet. I am not speaking of a New Age "oneness" that ignores basic class, status, and ethnic divisions in present-day society, divisions that must be resolved by radical social change. I am discussing the failure of today's Left to establish any affinity with a humane Left That Was, one that celebrated our potential for creating a shared humanity and civilization.

I realize only too well that these remarks will be viewed by many contemporary leftists as unsatisfactory. But in the Left That Was, the working class was at least seen (however erroneously) as the "non-class class" — that is, as a particular class that was obliged by inherent tendencies in capitalism to express the *universal* interests of humanity as well as its potentiality to create a rational society. This notion at least assumed that there were universal human interests that could be substantiated and realized under socialism, communism, or anarchism. Today's Left is "deconstructing" this appeal to universality to a point where it denies its validity and opposes reason itself on the basis that it is purely analytical and "unfeeling." What has been carried over to our time from the sixties is a basically uncritical assortment of narrow interests — and, one is obliged to add, alluring university careers — that have reduced universalistic to particularistic concerns. The great ideal of an emancipated *humanity* — hopefully one in harmony with nonhuman nature — has been steadily eroded by particularistic claims to hegemonic roles for gender-biased, ethnic-biased, and other like tendencies.

These tendencies threaten to turn the Left back to a more parochial, exclusionary, and ironically, more hierarchical past insofar as one group, whether alone or in concert with others, affirms its superior qualifications to lead society and guide movements for social change. What many leftists today are destroying is a great tradition of human solidarity and a belief in the potentiality for humanness, one that transcends nationality, ethnicity, gender differences, and a politics of hegemonic superiority.

I cannot hope to deal here with all the details of the social idealism, humanism, and drive for theoretical coherence that made the Left That Was so different from the pap leftism that exists today. Instead, I should like to focus on the internationalist and confederalist tendencies, the democratic spirit, the anti-militarism, and the rational secularism that distinguished it from other political and social movements of our period.

INTERNATIONALISM, NATIONALISM, AND CONFEDERATION

THE NATIONALISM THAT PERMEATES much of the Left of the eighties and nineties (often in the name of "national liberation") was largely alien to the far-seeing leftists of the last century and the early part of the present one. In using the word *Left*, I am drawing from the language of the French Revolution of 1789-94 so that I can include various types of anarchist as well as socialist thought. The Left That Was not only established its pedigree in the French Revolution but defined itself in opposition to that revolution's shortcomings, such as the Jacobin message of "patriotism" (although even this "nationalistic" notion had its roots in the belief that France belonged to its people rather than to the King of France — who was obliged to change his title to the King of the French after 1789 as a result).

Repelled by the references of the French revolutionaries to *la patrie*, the Left That Was generally came to regard nationalism as a regressive, indeed, as a divisive force that separated human from human by creating national boundaries. The Left That Was saw *all* national boundaries as the barbed wire that compartmentalized human beings by dividing them according to particularistic loyalties and commitments that obscured the domination of all oppressed people by ruling strata.

To Marx and Engels, the subjugated of the world had no country. They had only their international solidarity to sustain them, their unity as a class that was historically destined to remove class society as such. Hence the ringing conclusion of *The Communist Manifesto*: "Working Men of All Countries, Unite!" And in the body of that work (which the anarchist Mikhail Bakunin translated into Russian), we are told: "In the national struggles of the proletarians of different countries, [Communists] point out and bring to the front the common interests of the entire proletariat, independently of all nationality."

Further, the *Manifesto* declares, "The working men have no country. We cannot take away from them what they have not got." To the extent that Marx and Engels did give their support to some national liberation struggles, it was largely from their concerns about matters of geopolitics and economics or even for sentimental reasons, as in the case of Ireland, rather than principle. They supported the Polish national movement, for example, primarily because they wanted to weaken the Russian Empire, which in their day was the supreme counterrevolutionary power on the European continent. And they wished to see a united Germany, arguing (very wrongly, in my view) that the nation-state was desirable in providing the best arena for the development of capitalism, which they regarded as historically progressive (again wrongly, in my view). But never did they impute any virtues to nationalism as an end in itself.

Specifically, it was Frederick Engels, a popularizer and also a vulgarizer of Marx's thought, who regarded the nation-state as "the normal political constitution of the European bourgeoisie" in a letter to Karl Kautsky, barely a month before the physically debilitated Marx died. Dealing as it did with Poland's struggle for independence from Russia, Engels's letter advanced what Paul Nettl has called a "narrow preoccupation" with the "resurrection" of the country. This letter later created a great deal of mischief in the Marxist movement: it provided self-proclaimed

Marxist parties like the German Social-Democratic Party with an excuse to support their own country in August 1914, which subsequently destroyed proletarian internationalism during World War I.

But even within the Marxist movement, Engels's "narrow preoccupation" with nationalism did not go unchallenged in the pre-1914 era. Rosa Luxemburg's refusal to bow to nationalist tendencies in the Polish Socialist Party was of outstanding importance in perpetuating the internationalist legacy of socialism — she was no less a leading voice in that party than she was in the German Social-Democratic Party and the Second International generally. Her general views were consistently revolutionary: the socialist ideal of achieving a common humanity, she held, was incompatible with nationalist parochialism. As early as 1908, Luxemburg wrote:

> Speaking of the right of nations to self-determination we dispense *with the idea of a nation as a whole.* It becomes merely a social and political unity [for the purposes of measurement]. But it was just this concept of nations as one of the categories of bourgeois ideology that Marxist theory attacked most fiercely, pointing out under slogans like "national self-determination" or "freedom of the citizen," "equality before the law" — there lurks all the time a twisted and limited meaning. In a society based on classes, the nation as a uniform social-political whole simply does not exist. Instead, there exists within each nation classes with antagonistic interests and "rights." There is literally no social arena — from the strongest material relationship to the most subtle moral one — in which the possessing classes and a self-conscious proletariat could take one and the same position and figure as one undifferentiated national whole. (emphasis added)

She expressed these views most sharply with reference to the Russian, Ottoman, Austro-Hungarian, and other empires of the day, and she gained a sizable number of supporters in the socialist movement as a whole. As it turned out, I may note,

Luxemburg was bitterly opposed on this point by two of the most insipid vulgarizers of Marx's theories — Karl Kautsky of the German Social-Democratic Party and George Plekhanov of the Russian Social-Democratic Party, not to speak of activists like Josef Pilsudski, of the Polish Socialist Party, who was to become the notorious "strongman" of Poland during the inter-war period. It was Lenin, in particular, who supported "national struggles" largely for opportunistic reasons and for notions that stem from Engels's view of the nation-state as historically "progressive."

Anarchists were even more hostile than many Marxist socialists in their opposition to nationalism. Anarchist theorists and activists opposed the formation of nation-states everywhere in the world, a view that placed them politically far in advance of the Marxists. Any approval of the nation-state, much less a centralized entity of any kind, ran contrary to anarchist antistatism and its commitment to a universalized conception of humanity.

Bakunin's views on the subject of nationalism were very forthright. Without denying the right of every cultural group, indeed the "smallest folk-unit," to enjoy the freedom to exercise its own rights as a community, he warned:

> We should place human, universal justice above all national interests. And we should abandon the false principle of nationality, invented of late by the despots of France, Russia, and Prussia for the purpose of crushing the sovereign principle of liberty. . . . Everyone who sincerely wishes peace and international justice, should once and for all renounce the glory, the might, and the greatness of the Fatherland, should renounce all egoistic and vain interests of patriotism.

In sharp opposition to the state's preemption of societal functions of coordination, anarchist theorists advanced the fundamental notion of confederation, in which communes or municipalities in various regions could freely unite by means of recallable delegates. The functions of these confederal delegates were strictly administrative. Policy-making was to be left to the communes or municipalities themselves (although there was no clear agreement among anarchists on how the decision-making process was to function).

Nor was confederalism—as an alternative to nationalism and statism—a purely theoretical construct. Historically, confederalism and statism had been in conflict with each other for centuries. This conflict reached back to the distant past, but it erupted very sharply throughout the era of the democratic and proletarian revolutions, notably in the new United States during the 1780s, in France in 1793 and 1871, in Russia in 1921, and in the Mediterranean countries, notably Italy and Spain, in the nineteenth century — and again in Spain during the revolution of 1936.

In fact, Spanish anarchism, the largest of the anarchist movements in Europe, flatly opposed Catalan nationalism despite the fact that its largest following by the 1930s was recruited from the Catalan proletariat. So uncompromising were anarchist attempts to foster internationalism that clubs were formed everywhere among the Spanish anarchists to promote the use of Esperanto as a worldwide means of communication. Far more ethical than even Luxemburg, anarchists generally raised so-called "abstract rights" that were anchored in humanity's universality and solidarity, a vision that stood opposed to the institutional and ideological particularism that divided human from human.

THE COMMITMENT TO DEMOCRACY

THE LEFT THAT WAS viewed any abridgement of free expression as abhorrent and reactionary. With few exceptions (Lenin's views are a case in point), the entire Left of the nineteenth and early twentieth centuries was nourished by the ideals of "popular rule" and the radicalization of democracy, often in sharp reaction to the authoritarian rule that had marked the Jacobin phase of the French Revolution. (The word *democracy*, I should note, varied greatly in its meaning, ranging from free expression and assembly under republican institutions — the common socialist view — to face-to-face democracy — the common anarchist view.) Even Marx and Engels, who were by no means *democrats* in the sense of being committed to face-to-face democracy, wrote in *The Communist Manifesto* that "to raise the proletariat to the position of ruling class [is] to win the battle for democracy" — a clear avowal that "bourgeois democracy" was flawed in its scope and ideals. Indeed, the elimination of classes and class rule by the proletariat was expected to yield "an association, in which the free development of each is the free development of all" — an avowal that literally became a slogan comparable to "Working Men of All Countries, Unite!" and that persisted well into the Left of the 1930s.

As a Marxist, Luxemburg never strayed from this 1848 vision. In fact, her vision of revolution was integrally bound up with a proletariat that in her eyes was not only prepared to take power but was acutely knowledgeable of its humanistic task through experience and the give-and-take of free discussion. Hence her firm belief that revolution would be the work not of a party but of the proletariat itself. The role of the party, in effect, was to educate, not to command. In her critique of the Bolshevik Revolution, written only six months before she was murdered in the aftermath of the failed Spartacist uprising of January 1919, Luxemburg declared:

> Freedom only for the supporters of the [Bolshevik] government, only for the members of one party — however numerous they may be — is no freedom at all. Freedom is always and exclusively freedom for the one who thinks differently. Not because of any fanatical conception of "justice" but because all that is instructive, wholesome, and purifying in political freedom depends on this essential characteristic and its effectiveness vanishes when "freedom" becomes a special privilege.

Despite her support of the Russian Revolution, Luxemburg lashed out at Lenin over this issue as early as 1918 in the harshest terms:

> Lenin is completely mistaken in the means he employs. Decree, dictatorial force of the factory overseer, draconic penalties, rule by terror, all these things are but palliatives. The only way to rebirth is the school of public life itself, the most unlimited, the broadest de-

mocracy and public opinion. It is rule by terror which demoralizes.

And with very rare prescience for that time in the revolutionary movement, she warned that the proletarian dictatorship reduced to a mere elite would result in a "brutalization of public life," such as ultimately did occur under Stalinist rule.

> With the repression of political life in the land as a whole, life in the Soviets must also become crippled.... life dies out in every public institution, becomes a mere semblance of life, in which only the bureaucracy remains as the active element.

For the anarchists, democracy had a less formal and more substantive meaning. Bakunin, who was presumably contrasting his views with Rousseau's abstract conception of the citizen, declared:

> No, I have in mind only liberty worthy of that name, liberty consisting in the full development of all the material, intellectual, and moral powers latent in every man; a liberty which does not recognize any other restrictions but those which are traced by the laws of our own nature, which, properly speaking, is tantamount to saying that there are no restrictions at all, since these laws are not imposed upon us by some outside legislator standing above us or alongside us. Those laws are immanent, inherent in us; they constitute the very basis of our being, material as well as intellectual and moral; and instead of finding in them a limit to our liberty we should regard them as its real conditions and as its effective reason.

Bakunin's "liberty," in effect, is the fulfillment of humanity's potentiality and immanent tendency to achieve realization in an anarchist society. Accordingly, this "liberty ... far from finding itself checked by the freedom of others, is, on the contrary confirmed by it." Still further: "We understand by freedom from the positive point of view, the development, as complete as possible, of all faculties which man has within himself, and, from the negative point of view, the independence of the will of everyone from the will of others."

ANTIMILITARISM AND REVOLUTION

THE LEFT THAT WAS contained many pacifists, but its most radical tendencies eschewed nonviolence and committed themselves to *antimilitarism* rather than pacifism as a social as well as a combative issue. In their view, militarism implied a regimented society, a subordination of democratic rights in crisis situations such as war or, for that matter, revolution. Militarism inculcated obedience in the masses and conditioned them to the imperatives of a command society.

But what the Left That Was demanded was not the symbolic image of the "broken rifle" — so very much in vogue these days in pacifist boutiques —but the training and arming of the people for revolutionary ends, solely in the form of democratic militias. A resolution coauthored by Luxemburg and Lenin (a rare event) and adopted by the Second International in 1906 declared that it "sees in the democratic organization of the army, in the popular militia instead of the standing army, an essential guarantee for the prevention of aggressive wars, and for facilitating the removal of differences between nations."

This was not simply an antiwar resolution, although opposition to the war that was fast approaching was the principal focus of the statement. The arming of the people was a basic tenet of the Left That Was, and pious demands for gun control among today's leftists would have been totally alien to the thinking of the Left That Was. As recently as the 1930s, the concept of "the people in arms" remained a basic tenet of independent socialist, not to speak of anarchist, movements throughout the world, including those of the United States, as I myself so well remember. The notion of schooling the masses in reliance on the police and army for public safety, much less of turning the other cheek in the face of violence, would have been regarded as heinous.

Not surprisingly, revolutionary anarchists were even less ambiguous than socialists. In contrast to the state-controlled militia that the Second International was prepared to accept in the 1906 resolution cited above, the anarchists sought the direct arming of the masses. In Spain, weapons were supplied to anarchist militants from the very inception of the movement. The workers and peasants relied on themselves, not on the largess of statist institutions, to obtain the means for insurrection. Just as their notion of democracy meant direct democracy, so their notion of antimilitarism meant that they had to countervail the state's monopoly of violence with an armed popular movement — not merely a state-subsidized militia.

Secularism and Rationalism

It remains to add that anarchists and to a great extent the revolutionary socialists of the Left That Was not only tried to speak in the general interests of humanity but abjured any body of ideas and prejudices that denied humanity its naturalistic place in the scheme of things. They regarded the worship of deities as a form of subjugation to creations of human making, as the masking of reality by illusion, and as the manipulation of human fears, alienation, and anomie by calculated elites in behalf of an oppressive social order. Generally, the Left That Was boldly laid claim to the rationalist heritage of the Enlightenment and the French Revolution, however much this saddled the Marxists with mechanistic ideas. But also, organic forms of reason, borrowed from Hegel, competed with mechanism and conventional empiricism. Where intuitional notions competed with materialist ones among anarchists, they attracted a sizable body of artists to the anarchist movements of the past, or to anarchist ideas. Additionally, rationalism did not crowd out emotive approaches that fostered a highly moral socialism that was often indistinguishable from libertarian outlooks. But almost every attempt apart from certain individual exceptions was made to place mechanistic, organic, and emotive approaches to reality in a rational framework — notably, to achieve a *coherent* approach to social analysis and change.

That this endeavor led to disparate tendencies in the Left That Was should not surprise us. But the notion of a rational society achieved by rational as well as moral means and idealistic sentiments formed a unifying outlook for the Left That Was. Few leftists would have accepted William Blake's notion of reason as "meddlesome" or current postmodern views of coherence as "totalitarian."

The Left That Was was divided over the question of whether there could be a peaceful, indeed reformistic, evolution of capitalism into socialism or whether an insurrectionary break with the capitalist system was unavoidable. The wariness of the Left That Was toward reforms can perhaps best be seen in the fact that years ago, serious debates occurred among Western leftists of all kinds on whether they should fight for the eight-hour day, which many thought would make capitalism more palatable to the working class. In Tsarist Russia, the Left seriously debated whether their organizations should try to alleviate famine conditions among the peasantry lest their charitable efforts deflect the anger of the peasantry away from Tsarism.

But however serious those differences were, attempts at reform for its *own sake* were never part of leftist ideology. The *revolutionary* Left — which truly defined socialist and anarchist movements as a Left — certainly did not want to improve the capitalist system, much less give it a "human face." "Capitalism with a human face" was an expression they would have regarded as a contradiction in terms. The Left That Was hoped to overthrow capitalism and initiate a radically new social system, not to rationalize the existing order and make it acceptable to the masses.

To participate in struggles for reforms was seen as a means to *educate* the masses, not a way to dole out charity or improve their material lot. Demands for reforms were always permeated by the broader message that fundamental social reconstruction was needed. The fight for the eight-hour day, years ago, and strikes for better living conditions, not to speak of legislative improvements for working people, were seen as means for mobilizing the oppressed, for engaging them in struggles, and for disclosing the limits — and basic irrationalism — of capitalism, not simply or even significantly as a means for bettering life under capitalism. It was not until a later day that reforms were advocated by so-called leftist parties, candidates, deputies, and humane devotees of the working class, the poor, and the elderly as techniques for "humanizing" capitalism or rendering leftist candidates more popular — and electable for public office.

To ask for improved working and living conditions was seen as a way of directly challenging the "wage system" and the sovereignty of capital. Even so-called "evolutionary" or "reformist" socialists who hoped to ease from capitalism into socialism were revolutionary in the sense that they believed capitalism had to be replaced by a radically new social order. Their conflicts with the revolutionary socialists and anarchists in the Left That Was centered on whether capitalism *could* be replaced by piecemeal changes, not on whether it could be given a "human face." The First World War and particularly the revolutions that followed it left reformist socialism in debris — but it also produced a Left that radically departed in many of its basic tenets from the Left That Was.

THE FIRST WORLD WAR AND BOLSHEVISM

THE OUTBREAK OF THE FIRST WORLD WAR, the Bolshevik revolution of 1917, and the murder of Rosa Luxemburg and Karl Liebknecht in the Spartacus League uprising of January 1919 (a drawing of socialist blood that occurred with the indirect assent of the official German Social Democrats) opened a major breach in the history of the Left generally.

At the outbreak of the war, nearly all the socialist parties of warring Europe succumbed to nationalism, and their parliamentary fractions voted to give war credits to their respective capitalist states. Nor did the attitudes of certain leading anarchists, including Kropotkin, prove to be more honorable than those of the "social patriots," to use Lenin's epithet for the German and French socialist leaders who supported one or another camp in the war.

To analyze the reasons why this breach was opened in the Left That Was would require a study in itself. But the Bolshevik seizure of power in November 1917 did not close the breach. Quite to the contrary — it widened it, not only because of the unavoidable polarization of Bolshevism against Social Democracy but because of the authoritarian elements that had always formed a part of the highly conspiratorial Russian revolutionary movement. The Bolshevik party had little commitment to popular democracy. Lenin had never viewed "bourgeois democracy" as anything more than an instrument that could be used or discarded as expediency required. Many demands were placed on the largely Bolshevik regime that was formed in November (it initially included Left Social Revolutionaries as well): the advancing German army on the eastern front, the incredibly savage civil war that followed the Revolution, the isolation of the Bolsheviks from the workers and peasants in the early 1920s, and the attempt by the Kronstadt sailors to recover a soviet democracy that had been effaced by the bureaucratic Bolshevik party. These demands combined to bring out the worst features of Lenin's centralist views and his opportunistic views of democracy. Beginning in the early twenties, all affiliates of the Communist International were "Bolshevized" by Zinoviev and his Stalinist successors, until the commitment of socialism to democracy was marginalized and largely faded in the Communist parties of the world.

No less important in undermining the Left That Was were the various myths, popularized by Lenin, that capitalism had entered a unique, indeed "final" stage of its development, a stage marked by "imperialism" and worldwide "struggles for national liberation." Here, again, Lenin's position is too complex to be dealt with cursorily; but what is important is that the traditional internationalism that had marked the Left That Was increasingly gave way to an emphasis on "national liberation" struggles, partly for the purpose of weakening Western imperialism, and partly to foster economic development in colonized countries, thereby bringing the domestic class conflict within these countries to the top of their national agendas.

The Bolsheviks did not abandon the rhetoric of internationalism, to be sure, any more than the Social Democrats did. But "national liberation" struggles (which the Bolsheviks largely honored in the breach at home, after they took power in the newly formed Soviet Union) uncritically fostered a commitment by the Left to the formation of new nation-states. Nationalism increasingly came to the foreground of socialist theory and practice. It is not surprising that the first "People's Commissar of Nationalities" in the new Soviet Union was Joseph Stalin, who later fostered this nationalistic trend in Marxism-Leninism and who during and after the Second World War gave it a distinctly "patriotic" quality in the USSR. Expressions claiming that the Soviet Union was the "fatherland of the working class" were ubiquitous among Communists of the interwar period, and their parties were modeled on the centralized Bolshevik Party to allow for Stalin's blatant interference in their affairs.

By 1936, the politics of the Communist International (or what remained of it) had veered sharply away from the ideals that had once guided the Left That Was. Luxemburg, honored more as a martyr than as a theorist, was discredited by the Stalinist cabal or totally ignored. The Second International was essentially moribund. Idealism began to give way to a crudely amoral opportunism and to an antimilitarism that was variously emphasized, rejected, or modified to suit the foreign policy of the Stalinist regime.

Yet opposition there was — as late as 1939 — to this degeneration of the ideas that had defined the Left That Was — opposition from left-wing tendencies in certain socialist parties, from anarchists, and from dissident Communist groups. The Left That Was did not disappear without furious debates over these ideals or without attempts to retain its historic premises. Its ideals remained at the top of the revolutionary agenda during the entire interwar period, not only as a source of polemics but as part of an armed confrontation in the Spanish Revolution of 1936. Leftist parties and groups still agonized over issues like internationalism, democracy, antimilitarism, revolution, and their relationship to the state — agonies that led to furious intramural and interparty conflicts. These issues were branded on the entire era before they began to fade — and their fading altered the very definition of leftism itself.

THE LEFT AND THE "COLD WAR"

THE "COLD WAR" INVADED the humanistic agenda of the Left That Was by turning most leftist organizations into partisans of the West or the East and by introducing a dubious "anti-imperialism" into what became Cold War politics. "National liberation" became the virtual centerpiece of the "New Left" and of the aging "Old Left," at least their various Stalinist, Maoist, and Castroist versions.

It should be understood — as this Left did not — that imperialism is not unique to capitalism. As a means of exploitation and cultural homogenization, and as a source of tribute, it existed throughout the ancient, medieval, and early modern eras. In ancient times the imperial hegemony of Babylon was followed by that of Rome and the medieval Holy Roman Empire. Indeed, throughout history there have been African, Indian, Asian, and in modern times, expansionist and exploitative "subimperialist" states that were more precapitalist than capitalist in character. If "war is the health of the state," war has usually meant expansionism (read: imperialism) among the more commanding states of the world and even among their client states.

In the early part of the twentieth century, the various writings on imperialism by J. A. Hobson, Rudolf Hilferding, and Lenin, among others, did not discover the concept of imperialism. They simply added new, uniquely capitalist features to earlier characterizations of imperialism, such as the "export of capital" and the impact of capitalism on the economic development of colonized countries. But what capitalism has also exported with a vengeance, in addition to capital itself, has been nationalism (not only demands for cultural autonomy) and nationalism in the form of centralized nation-states. Indeed, the centralized nation-state has been exported to peoples who might more reasonably have turned to confederal forms of struggle and social reconstruction in asserting their cultural uniqueness and right to self-management. Let me emphasize that my criticisms of nationalism and statism are not meant to reject the genuine aspirations of cultural groups for full expression and self-governance. This is particularly the case where attempts are made to subvert their cultural uniqueness and their rights to freedom. The issue with which I am concerned is how their cultural autonomy is expressed and the *institutional structures* they establish to manage themselves as unique cultural entities. The cultural integrity of a people does not have to be embodied in the form of a nation-state. It should, in my view, be expressed in forms that retain valuable cultural traditions and practices in confederal institutions of self-management. It was goals such as these in particular that were raised and prized by the great majority of anarchists and libertarian socialists, even certain Marxists, in the Left That Was.

What has happened instead is that the export of the nation-state has poisoned not only the modern Left but the human condition itself. In recent years, "Balkanization" and parochialism have become vicious phenomena of disastrous proportions. The recent and much-described breakup of the Russian empire has resulted in bloody national struggles and aspirations for state-formation that are pitting culturally disparate communities against each other in ways that threaten to regress to barbarism. The internationalist ideals that the Left That Was advanced, particularly in the former "socialist bloc," have been replaced by an ugly parochialism — directed against Jews generally and in much of Europe against "foreign workers" from all parts of the world. In the Near East, Africa, Asia, and Latin America, colonized or formerly colonized peoples have developed imperial appetites of their own, so that many of what now pass for former colonies that have been liberated from Euro-American imperialist powers are now pursuing brutally imperialist aspirations of their own.

For the emergence of an authentic Left what is disastrous here is that leftists in the United States and Europe often condone appalling behavior on the part of former colonies, in the name of "socialism," "anti-imperialism," and of course "national liberation." The present-day Left is no less a victim of the "Cold War" than colonized peoples who were pawns in it. Leftists have all but jettisoned the ideals of the Left That Was, and in so doing, they have come to accept a kind of client status of their own — first, in the 1930s, as supporters of the "workers' fatherland" in the East, and more recently as supporters of former colonies bent on their own imperialist adventures.

What matters is not whether such leftists in Europe or the United States do or do not support "liberated" nation-states that are either newly emerging, subimperialist, or imperialist. Whether Western leftists "support" these nation-states and their endeavors means as much to those states as seagull-droppings on an ocean shore. Rather, what really matters — and what is the more serious tragedy — is that these leftists rarely ask whether peoples they support accept statist regimes or confederal associations, whether they oppress other cultures, or whether they oppress their own or other populations — let alone whether they themselves should be supporting a nation-state at all.

Indeed, many leftists fell into the habit of opposing the imperialism of the superpowers in a mere reaction to the sides that were lined up in the "Cold War." This "Cold War" mentality persists even after the "Cold War" has come to an end. More than ever, leftists today are obliged to ask if their "anti-imperialist" and "national liberation" concerns help to foster the emergence of *more* nation-states and *more* ethnic and "subimperialist" rivalries. They must ask, what character is anti-imperialism taking today? Is it validating ethnic rivalries, the emergence of domestic tyrannies, subimperialist ambitions, and a rapacious collection of militaristic regimes?

Clearly, parochialism is one product of the new "anti-imperialist" nationalism and statism that has been nourished by the "Cold War" and the reduction of specious leftists to minions of old Stalinist and Maoist-type conflicts dressed in the garb of "national liberation." Parochialism can also function internally, partly as an extension of the "Cold War" into domestic spheres of life. Self-styled spokespeople for ethnic groups who literally pit one racial group against another, dehumanizing (for whatever reason) one to enhance the other; spokespeople for gender groups that parallel such exclusionary ethnic groups in opposition to their sexual counterparts; spokespeople for religious groups that do the same with respect to other religious groups — all reflect atavistic developments that would have had no place in the Left That Was. That the *rights* of ethnic, gender, and like strata of a given population must be cherished and that cultural distinctions must be prized is not in question here. But apart from the justified claims of all these groups, their aims should be sought within a human-oriented framework, not within an exclusionary or parochial folk-oriented one. If an authentic Left is once again to emerge, the myth of a "hegemonic" group of oppressed people, which seeks to rearrange human relations in a new hierarchical pyramid, must be replaced by the goal of achieving an ethics of complementarity in which differences enrich the whole. In ancient times, the slaves of Sicily who revolted and forced all free men to fight as gladiators in the island's amphitheaters behaved no differently from their masters. They reproduced what was still a slave culture, replacing one kind of slave with another.

Moreover, if there is to be a Left that in any sense resembles the Left That Was, it cannot be merely "left of center." Liberalism — with its menu of small reforms that obscure the irrationality of the prevailing society and make it more socially acceptable — is an arena in its own right. Liberalism has no "left" that can be regarded as its kin or its critical neighbor. The Left must stake out its own arena, one that stands in revolutionary opposition to the prevailing society, not one that participates as a "leftist" partner in its workings.

WILL THERE BE A LEFT TODAY?

CERTAINLY THE LEFT THAT WAS FOUGHT against innumerable irrationalities in the existing social order, such as long debilitating working hours, desperate hunger, and abject poverty. It did so because the perpetuation of these irrationalities would have completely demoralized the forces fighting for basic social change. It often raised seemingly "reformist" demands, but it did so to reveal the *failure* of the existing social order to meet the most elementary needs of denied people. In fighting for these "reforms," however, the concern of the Left That Was was explicitly and unwaveringly focused on the need to change the whole social order, not on making it less irrational and more palatable. Today, the Left That Was would have also fought with desperation against the forces that are depleting the ozone layer, destroying forests, and proliferating nuclear power plants in order to *preserve life itself* on this planet.

By the same token, however, the Left That Was recognized that there are many problems that *cannot* be solved within the framework of capitalism. It held, however "unrealistically" it may seem, to its revolutionary position rather than curry public favor or surrender its identity to opportunistic programs. At any given moment, history does not always present the Left with clear-cut alternatives or immediately "effective" courses of action. In August 1914, for example, no forces existed that could have prevented the outbreak of World War I, not even the Social Democracy that had committed itself to opposition to the war. The Left had to live an ineffectual, often hidden, frustrating life amidst the effluvium of popular jingoism that engulfed so much of Europe, including most of the workers in the socialist movement itself. Similarly, in 1938, there was no longer any possibility that the Spanish Revolution could be rescued from fascist military attacks and insidious Stalinist counterrevolution, despite the valiant struggles that continued for the greater part of a year thereafter.

Regrettably, there are some impossible situations in which an authentic Left can only take a moral stance, with no hope of intervening successfully. In such cases, the Left can only patiently try to educate those who are willing to listen, to advance its ideas to rational individuals, however small their numbers may be, and to act as an ethical force in opposition to the "art of the possible," to use a famous liberal definition of politics. A recent case in point was an admirable slogan that was raised at the inception of the Gulf War, namely "Neither Side Is Right" — a slogan that obviously did not resonate with the nationalistic attitude of the great majority of American people, nor one that was likely to be politically effective. Indeed, to choose sides in the Gulf War would have been to confuse American national chauvinism with democracy, on the one hand, or to confuse an indifference to Saddam Hussein's totalitarianism with "anti-imperialism," on the other.

To pretend that an authentic Left can *always* offer a practical solution to every problem in society is chimerical. Offering "lesser evils" as a solution to every evil that this society generates will lead to the worst of all possible evils — the dissolution of the Left into a liberal morass of endless compromises and humiliations. Amid all its fights in support of concrete issues, an authentic Left advances the message that the present society must be demolished and replaced by one that is rational. Such was the case with socialists like Eugene V. Debs and anarchists like Emma Goldman and Alexander Berkman in the Left That Was. Put bluntly: What this society usually does should not deter leftists from probing the logic of events from a rational standpoint or from calling for what society *should* do. Any attempt to adapt the rational "should" to the irrational "is" vacates that space on the political spectrum that should be occupied by a Left premised on reason, freedom, and ecological humanism. The need to steadfastly maintain the principal commitments that minimally define a Left may not always be popular, but the alternative to the monstrous irrationalities that permeate present-day society must always be kept open, fostered, and developed if we are ever to achieve a free society.

It may well be that in the foreseeable future an authentic Left has little, if any, prospects of gaining a large following. But if it surrenders the most basic principles that define it — internationalism, democracy, antimilitarism, revolution, secularism, and rationalism — as well as others, like confederalism, the word *Left* will no longer have any meaning in our political vocabulary. One may call oneself a liberal, a social democrat, a "realo" Green, or a reformist. That is a choice that each individual is free to make, according to his or her social and political convictions. But for those who call themselves *leftists*, there should be a clear understanding that the use of the term Left involves the acceptance of the fundamental principles that literally define and justify the use of the word. This means that certain ideas like nationalism, parochialism, authoritarianism--and certainly, for anarchists of all kinds, any commitment to a nation-state — and symbols like the broken rifle of pacifism are totally alien to the principles that define the Left. Such ideas, introduced into politics, have no place in any politics that can authentically be characterized as leftist. If no such politics exists, the term *Left* should be permitted to perish with honor.

But if the Left were to finally disappear because of the melding of reformist, liberal, nationalist, and parochial views, not only would modern society lose the "principle of hope," to use Ernst Bloch's expression, an abiding principle that has guided all revolutionary movements of the past; the Left would cease to be the conscience of society. Nor could it advance the belief that the present society is totally irrational and must be replaced by one that is guided by reason, an ecological ethics, and a genuine concern for human welfare. For my part, that is not a world in which I would want to live.

— May 1991

Also Available from AK Distribution

A lifelong radical since the early 1930s, Murray Bookchin was a trade-union activist in the 1930s and 1940s, an innovative theorist in the 1960s, and a leading participant in the antinuclear movement and the radical wing of the Greens in the 1970s and 1980s. Now in his seventies, Bookchin's writing have had a strong influence on left libertarians. All of his work currently in print is available mail-order from AK Distribution:

Ecology of Freedom: The Emergence And Dissolution Of Hierarchy - $19.95/£11.99, paperback, Black Rose. A new revised edition of his magnus opus. The most systematic articulation of his ideas - his "epistemology of liberation."

The Philosophy of Social Ecology - $18.95/£11.99, paperback, Black Rose. The latest set of essays on "dialectical naturalism."

Defending the Earth: A Dialogue Between Murray Bookchin and Dave Foreman - $10.00/£8.95, paperback, South End. Essays from their "great debate."

Post-Scarcity Anarchism - 18.95/£11.99, paperback, Black Rose. A seminal collection of essays on anarchism, ecology, appropriate technology and the anti-nuclear movement. Includes the classic "Listen Marxist."

Remaking Society: Pathways to a Green Future - $10.00/£8.95, paperback, South End. A primer on Bookchin"s ideas, taking the reader through anthropology, the emergence of hierarchy and modern capitalism, technology, utopian radical solutions, urbanization and communities, and the ethics of social ecology.

The Limits of the City - 17.95/£11.99, paperback, Black Rose. A history of city life which, once progressive, has reached its "ultimate negation in the modern metropolis."

The Modern Crisis - $9.95/£8.95, paperback, New Society. A primer of social ecology, and perhaps the most concise and approachable introduction to Bookchin"s ideas.

Towards An Ecological Society - $18.95/£11.99, paperback, Black Rose. A classic collection of essays, including critiques of the environmental movement, explorations of the emancipatory possibilities for "ecocommunities and eco-technology", critiques of Marxism, and much more.

Urbanization Without Cities: The Rise and Decline of Citizenship - $19.95/ £11.99, paperback, Black Rose. The struggle for an environmentally-oriented politics, a new ecological ethics and a citizenry that will restore the balance between city and country, humanity and nature.

Deep Ecology And Anarchism - $5.95/£2.50, paperback, Freedom. A debate (with Graham Purchase, Brian Morris and Rodney Aitchtey) on deep ecology, social ecology and anarchism.

Customers in Britain and Europe, please send your order to our UK address. Customers in North America or outside Europe, please send your order to our US address.

North America Ordering Information: please add $2 postage for the first title, and 50¢ for each subsequent title. For international orders, please add $4 for the first title, and 50¢ for each subsequent title. Payment must be made by check (drawn on a US bank), money order, or international money order made payable to AK Press in US dollars. Please send all orders to: AK Press, P.O. Box 40682, San Francisco, CA 94140-0682.

British and European Ordering Information: Postage for Britain and Europe is £1.00 for the first item, and 50p for each additional item. Payment must be made by check (drawn on a UK bank), money order, or international money order made out to AK Retail in Pounds Sterling. Please send all orders to: AK Press, 22 Lutton Place, Edinburgh, Scotland, EH8 9PE, Great Britain.

A new CD recording from AK Press

AK PRESS AUDIO

NOAM CHOMSKY
THE CLINTON VISION

AK Audio, the newly formed audio imprint of AK Press, was created in order to bring the excitement and immediacy of the spoken word to people who care about politics. Reasonably priced, timely, and available on high-quality compact disc, **AK Audio** recordings deliver the best in political speech.

As an inaugural release, **AK Audio** makes Noam Chomsky, popular speaker, linguist, author, and political commentator, available to the home audience for the first time ever on compact disc. In 1992 Bill Clinton was elected President of the United States. After 12 years of a Republican White House, voters hungry for change believed Clinton when he promised a new vision, a new activism, and a new direction for the US. In **The Clinton Vision,** Noam Chomsky speaks about the US President's actions on NAFTA, health care, crime, labor relations, foreign policy, and the economy.

> *"Chomsky has been unrelenting in his attacks on the American hierarchy. . . . [He] is up there with Thoreau and Emerson in the literature of rebellion."* — *Rolling Stone*

> *"If the job of a rebel is to tear down the old and prepare for the new, then this is Noam Chomsky, a 'rebel without a pause,' the 'Elvis of academia. . . .' As rock 'n roll in the 90s continues to be gagged, it is ironic that a man of 65 years turns out to be the real rebel spirit."* — *U2's Bono*

> *"How adroitly [Chomsky] cuts through the crap and actually says something."* — *Village Voice*

ISBN 1-873176-92-9; $12.98/£10.99; CD; 56 minutes; two-color cover. **The Clinton Vision** CD is available direct from AK Press for $12.98/£10.99 ppd.

Friends
of AK Press

In the last 12 months, AK Press has published around 15 new titles. In the next 12 months we should be able to publish roughly the same, including new work by Murray Bookchin, CRASS, Daniel Guerin, Noam Chomsky, Jello Biafra, Stewart Home, a new anthology of situationist writings, new audio work from Noam Chomsky, plus more. However, not only are we financially constrained as to what (and how much) we can publish, we already have a huge backlog of excellent material we would like to publish sooner, rather than later. If we had the money, we could easily publish 30 titles in the coming 12 months.

Projects currently being worked on include a collection of essays by Nestor Makhno; previously unpublished early anarchist writings by Victor Serge; more work from Noam Chomsky, Murray Bookchin and Stewart Home; Raoul Vaneigem on the surrealists; a new anthology of computer hacking and hacker culture; a short history of British Fascism; the collected writings of Guy Aldred; a new anthology of cutting edge radical fiction and poetry; an updated version of the seminal anthology of contemporary anarchist writings, *Re-Inventing Anarchy*; new work from Freddie Baer; Albert Meltzer's autobiography and an updated reprint of *The Floodgates of Anarchy*; the autobiography and political writings of former Black Panther and class war prisoner Lorenzo Kom'boa Ervin, and much, much more. As well as working on the new AK Press Audio series, we are also working to set up a new pamphlet series, both to reprint long neglected classics and to present new material in a cheap, accessible format.

Friends of AK Press is a way in which you can directly help us try to realize many more such projects, much faster. Friends pay a minimum of $15/£10 per month into our AK Press account. All moneys received go directly into our publishing. In return, Friends receive (for the duration of their membership), automatically, as and when they appear, one copy free of every new AK Press title. Secondly, they are also entitled to 10 percent discount on everything featured in the current AK Distribution mail-order catalog (upwards of 3,000 titles), on any and every order. **Friends,** if they wish, can be acknowledged as a **Friend** in all new AK Press titles.

To find out more on how to contribute to Friends of AK Press, and for a Friends order form, please do write to:

AK Press	AK Press
PO Box 40682	22 Lutton Place
San Francisco, CA	Edinburgh, Scotland
94140-0682	EH8 9PE

Some Recent Titles from AK Press

THE STRUGGLE AGAINST THE STATE AND OTHER ESSAYS by Nestor Makhno. ISBN 1 873176 78 3; 128pp two color cover, perfect bound 5-1/2 x 8-1/2; £7.95/$9.95. Makhno was the leader of the anarchist/libertarian peasant army/insurrection, who successfully fought the Whites and the Bolsheviks, killed the bourgeoisie, and put anarchism into practice in the years following the Russian Revolution. This volume comprises various essays and articles written while Makhno was in exile in Paris in the 1920s.

ECOFASCISM: LESSONS FROM THE GERMAN EXPERIENCE by Janet Biehl and Peter Staudenmaier. ISBN 1 873176 73 2; 80pp two color cover, perfect bound 5-1/2 x 8-1/2; £5.00/$7.00. Two essays, "Fascist Ideology: The Green Wing of the Nazi Party and its Historial Anatecedents" and "Ecology and the Modernization of Fascism in the German Ultra-Right," along with a new introduction. "Taken together, these essays examine aspects of German fascism, past and present, in order to draw lessons from them for ecology movements both in Germany and elsewhere." [from the introduction]

TELEVISIONARIES: THE RED ARMY FACTION STORY 1963 TO 1993 BY TOM VAGUE; ISBN 1 873176 47 3; 112PP TWO COLOR COVER; PERFECT BOUND 5-1/2 x 8-1/2; £4.50/$6.95. An irreverent chronological history and analysis of the terrorist group that have shot and bombed their way through the last three decades.

END TIME: NOTES ON THE APOCALYPSE by G.A. Matiasz; ISBN 1873176 96 1; 320 pp four color cover, perfect bound 5-1/2 x 8-1/2; £5.95/$7.00. A first novel by G.A. Matiasz, an original voice of slashing, thought provoking style. "A compulsively readable thriller combined with a very smart meditation on the near-future of anarchism, *End Time* proves once again that science fiction is our only literature of ideas." — Hakim Bey

ECSTATIC INCISIONS: THE COLLAGES OF FREDDIE BAER by Freddie Baer, preface by Peter Lamborn Wilson; ISBN 1 873176 60 0; 80 pages, a three color cover, perfect bound 8 1/2 x 11; £7.95/$11.95. This is Freddie Baer's first collection of collage work; over the last decade her illustrations have appeared on numerous magazine covers, posters, t-shirts, and album sleeves. Includes collaborations with Hakim Bey, T. Fulano, Jason Keehn, and David Watson.

STEALWORKS: THE GRAPHIC DETAILS OF JOHN YATES by John Yates; ISBN 1 873176 51 1; 136 pp two color cover, perfect bound 8-1/2 x 11; £7.95/$11.95. A collection to date of work created by a visual mechanic and graphic surgeon. His work is a mixture of bold visuals, minimalist to-the-point social commentary, involves the manipulation and reinterpretation of culture's media imagery.

AK Press publishes and distributes a wide variety of radical literature. For our latest catalog featuring these and several thousand other titles, please send a large self-addressed, stamped envelope to:

AK Press
22 Lutton Place
Edinburgh, Scotland
EH8 9PE, Great Britain

AK Press
P.O. Box 40682
San Francisco, CA
94140-0682

.

Lightning Source UK Ltd.
Milton Keynes UK
UKHW041024140920
369870UK00002B/121